Reproduced by Permission of the Author

SCIPIO UNITED METHODIST

Reproduced by Permission of the Author

You *can* be like Jesus

by Sammy Tippit
as told to
Jerry Jenkins

VICTOR BOOKS
a division of SP Publications, Inc., Wheaton, Illinois
Offices also in Fullerton, California • Whitby, Ontario, Canada • London, England

Bible quotations are from the *New American Standard Bible,* © 1960, 1962, 1963, 1968, 1971, 1972, 1973, 1975, The Lockman Foundation. Other Bibles used are: *The Living Bible* (LB), © 1971, Tyndale House; *The New International Version* (NIV), © 1978, The New York International Bible Society. Used by permission.

Library of Congress Catalog Card Number: 79-63914
ISBN: 0-88207-579-9

© 1979, SP Publications, Inc. All rights reserved.
Printed in the United States of America.

VICTOR BOOKS
A division of SP Publications, Inc.
P.O. Box 1825 • Wheaton, Ill. 60187

Reproduced by Permission of the Author is designed for your personal reading pleasure and profit. It is also designed for group study. A leader's guide, with visual aids (SonPower Multiuse Transparency Masters) and Rip-Offs (student interaction booklets) are available from your local Christian bookstore or from the publisher.

Contents

1	The Goal of Discipleship: A Balanced Life	9
2	Humility: The Uncommon Denominator	19
3	Love that Doesn't Quit	31
4	Becoming like Jesus—in Prayer	45
5	What's the Good Word?	57
6	I Want to Tell the Whole World	67
7	Me, Be Crucified?	83
8	Let's Hear Your Battle Cry	91
9	Submit!	101
10	The Process of Growth	111
11	Spiritual Multiplying	125
12	The Cost of Being like Christ	133

1
The Goal of Discipleship: A Balanced Life

He was old enough to be my father. So when he challenged me to jog three miles with him the next morning, what could I say? *Why not?* I thought.

The next day I found out why not. By the time I had struggled to stay with him for half a mile, huffing and puffing and feeling as if my sides were about to split open, I had to beg off. "Bill," I gasped, "I can't do this. I've got to stop."

I was disappointed and disgusted to realize how out of shape I was. Just 30 years old, only 12 years since I had been a high school athlete, I couldn't run more than a half mile! I decided to set a goal. I wanted to run six miles in an average of seven minutes each.

Running every day, I gradually worked toward my goal. I ran three miles in 10 minutes each, and eventually I worked up to four miles at the same pace. As this is being written, I am up to six miles at seven and one-half minutes each, and I hope by the time this is printed to be at my goal.

I have gotten myself in shape, but it didn't happen in one day. It has taken months of work and determination and consistency. I set a goal and worked toward it.

If my running lapses, my body will get flabby and my minutes per mile will rise. I have to keep running to stay in shape.

If we have no goals, nothing to work toward in our Christian lives, we become spiritually flabby and out of shape. Too many of us are stumbling around, not knowing where we are going or where we should go. We've received Jesus Christ and asked Him to forgive our sins; but practically speaking, we don't know the real goal of the Christian life.

We are weak and feeble—as I was as a runner—till we realize our goal and start working toward it. The Bible says that goal is to be like Jesus. We should try to become like Him.

The Bible says, "From the very beginning God decided that those who came to Him—and all along He knew who would—should become like His Son, so that His Son would be the first, with many brothers" (Romans 8:29, LB). God's plan was not just to save people from death, but to transform them into the image of Jesus.

That transformation doesn't happen all at once, any more than my getting in shape happened in one day of running. Certainly, when we received Christ we became new creatures and God saw to it that we belonged to Him. But the molding and shaping of our beings into the image of Jesus is a process. We need to let the Holy Spirit help us grow.

Jesus Himself had goals in a sense. Everything He did—every word, action, and thought—was geared toward that ultimate purpose of His life, that of dying for the sins of mankind. Frequently He kept in touch with His Father, working toward the long-range plan of dying on the cross, being buried, and rising for the purchase of our salvation.

Jesus and John

Like Jesus, John the Baptist immersed himself in the Lord's work. His fame as a godly person continued even after he was beheaded by Herod's executioner.

John's life left a strong impression on the minds of those around him. When Herod heard of Jesus' teachings, he thought John had come back to life in the body of Jesus.

We have the potential to become like Christ as John was like Him, once we have received Him as our personal Saviour. We are to be in the world as Jesus is (1 John 4:17). What a job. What a responsibility. We are to live our daily lives so people will see Him in us.

Have you ever met anyone whose life reminded you of Jesus'? I have. A few years ago, I met Dr. Frank Laubach, a man known throughout the world as an educator of the illiterate and also as a deep man of prayer.

He immediately impressed me with his Christlikeness. For years he tried to demonstrate love, compassion, wisdom, and truth as the Lord did. Dr. Laubach was an old man then and has since died. But meeting him was a rich experience. I felt I had been in the actual presence of God who was at work in a man's life.

Jesus Is the Example of the Perfectly Balanced Life

How can we reflect the life of Jesus through our day-to-day, problem-filled lives? What characteristics of Him must we have before people will see Him in and through us? We can get a few clues toward becoming more like Jesus by looking at one of His personality traits: balance. Jesus is the most balanced and mature Person who ever lived.

Jesus balanced the characteristics of justice and forgiveness. When men wanted to stone a woman caught cheating on her husband, He forgave her. When money changers made a mockery of the temple, His Father's house, Jesus' anger was kindled; He carried out justice by driving them away.

He was also balanced in His approach to reaching people. Many times in the Scriptures we see Him dealing with people one-on-one—the woman at the well, Zaccheus, the blind man. At other times we see Him in small groups, as with the 10 lepers, or throughout the Gospels with His twelve disciples. On occasion He spoke to thousands. This balanced approach shoots holes in the theories of men who say a one-on-one approach is the only way to talk about the Good News, and also that of men who say mass evangelism is the only way.

Jesus was also balanced in His prayer and Scripture reading. He sought God frequently; yet He also memorized Scripture. When Satan tempted Him, He quoted the Word of God.

Even His death and resurrection show what a balanced Person He was. His death proved that Christians are not guaranteed of escaping suffering. In fact, the Apostle Paul wrote of sharing in the sufferings of Christ (2 Corinthians 1:5-7). Yet Christ's resurrection speaks to us of our hope and the power of God that is ours.

Roadblocks to Becoming like Christ

Some areas of our lives may be easier than others to balance. Some people have little trouble sharing their faith but have problems keeping up with their Bible study and praying. Others are fantastic at private devotions but unable to muster the courage to share their faith.

We may also have trouble becoming like Him because we lack patience. The Christlike life doesn't happen overnight. People who cruise around from experience to experience and meeting to meeting are looking for the highs of the Christian life so they can "get" one and ride it for a while. Are they becoming Christlike? No, they are trying a shortcut. They want something for nothing, the easy route.

Another roadblock to true discipleship and the balanced Christian life is extremism. This is the problem of grabbing onto *a* truth about God and excluding *the* truth, the *whole* truth about Him. Jesus says that He is the Truth (John 14:6). The danger in extremism lies in making a major point out of a minor one. One fruit of the Spirit (Galatians 5:22-23) is self-control. When our lives are brought under the guidance of the Holy Spirit, we have the self-discipline to avoid extremes. The more balanced we become, the more we become like Jesus.

When our organization, God's Love in Action, was based in Chicago, we ministered in the ghettos,

14 / Reproduced by Permission

working with drug addicts, gang leaders, runaways, and all sorts of other troubled young people. We held frequent Bible studies so the new converts could be trained in the Word of God and also so newcomers and the curious could be exposed to Christianity.

One night, during one of our Bible studies, a Christian layman visited and tried to witness to an unsaved gang leader who had come out of curiosity. This well-meaning layman told the tough guy that all he had to do to go to heaven was to confess with his mouth that Jesus was Lord and that God had raised Jesus from the dead.

"OK," the gang leader said, "Jesus is Lord and God raised Him from the dead."

The Goal of Discipleship / 15

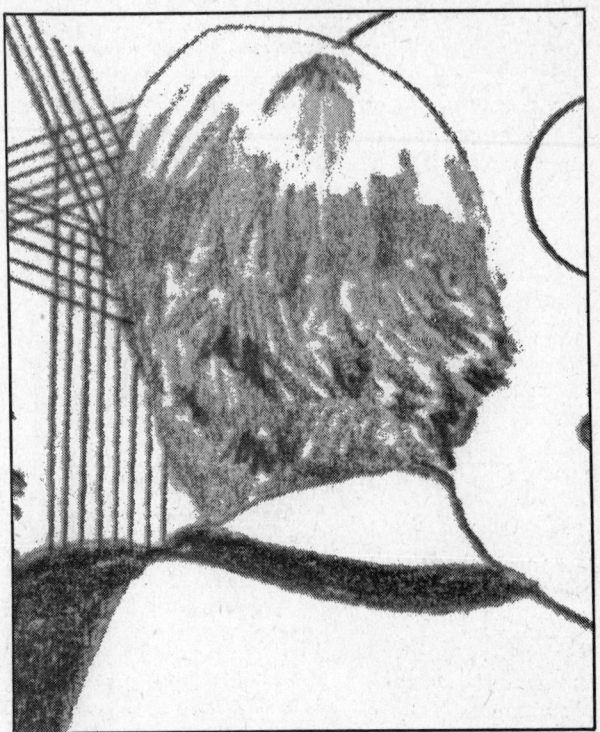

He was almost mocking the layman, but the man began running through our house, rejoicing that he led the gang leader to Christ. "He's a born-again Christian!" the man said.

But what had happened in the young tough's life? Nothing. In fact, worse than nothing. He had been turned off. And he was no better than when he had walked in the door. Before he left he told me that Christianity didn't work. He never came back. He was disgusted. Why? Because he had been given a partial truth that was not *the* whole truth. According to Paul's writing in Romans 10:9, if you confess with your mouth the Lord Jesus and *believe in your heart* that God has raised Him from the dead, you'll be saved.

That's a major difference. Could anyone who simply said the words become a child of God? No, the Bible doesn't say that. It would cheapen the Gospel. A person could almost become a Christian by accident! But the Bible says you must believe in your heart.

When we don't have the balance of the whole truth of faith and repentance, we are open to the dangerous weird teachings that are rampant today, many of which began by someone's overemphasizing a truth.

Truman Herring, a pastor friend, shared with me an appropriate example of this point. Say I make a drawing of your face, so perfect that every detail is accurate. Every hair and line is represented, except that your ears are each a foot long. Even if the rest of the drawing is perfectly accurate, you'd find yourself looking at a monster. By blowing one feature out of proportion, I have created a freak.

This is how many get a monstrous picture of Jesus Christ. They've latched onto one aspect of His truth and life and have blown it out of proportion. The balance is gone.

Probably the biggest hindrance to Christlike balance in our lives is the failure to gauge our spiritual intake and output. If all we do is take and take and take through church meetings, Christian concerts, Bible studies, fellowshipping with friends, and similar activities, we will become fat, lazy, intake-oriented Christians.

After I graduated from high school, went to college, got married and became a father, I found myself less and less physically active. In ten years I shot up from 155 pounds to just under 200. Yet when I tried to decrease my intake of food, I suffered headaches. You see, the problem wasn't that I was taking too much in. It was that I wasn't burning it off. I wasn't using it in energy. When I began to work out and exercise and ride a bike and jog, the pounds melted away.

If you are imbalanced by taking in too much spiritual food, the answer may not lie in cutting the intake. You may need to speed up your output. Learn to share your faith and exercise it. We'll talk about the hows in later chapters.

Finally, another major hindrance to becoming a balanced Christian is copying an attractive spiritual personality. Maybe the person is a flashy speaker or youth leader or even a pastor or Sunday School teacher. These people are valuable gifts from God to help us grow, but where are we when they fail us? Does our faith ooze down the drain with them? Not if they have really led us to Jesus Christ.

It's all right to admire other Christians and Christian leaders. And it is wonderful when God sends someone who pours his life into ours and we grow spiritually from it. But Jesus Christ Himself is our Model and Standard, and it is in Him alone that we can find fulfillment and balance.

2
Humility: The Uncommon Denominator

Have you ever tried to carry on a conversation with ants? You can shout at them, block their paths, or use sign language. But you can never really communicate with them unless you become an ant.

Jesus became a man so He could share His love for us. That's humility. And to become like Him, we have to be humble.

Since we can't become ants—or anything different from what we are—how do we get humble? What sort of life-style should we be shooting for?

God had to take me through many difficult things to teach me how important humility is for Christians.

Jesus' Humility

Humility is what Jesus' life is all about. The Bible tells us to be like Him. Paul wrote to his Christian brothers: "Have this attitude in yourselves which was also in Christ Jesus, who, though He existed in the form of God, did not regard equality with God a thing to be grasped, but emptied Himself, taking the form of a bond servant, and being made in the likeness of men. And being found in appearance as a man, He humbled Himself by becoming obedient to the point of death, even death on a cross. Therefore also God highly exalted Him, and bestowed on Him the name which is above every name" (Philippians 2:5-9).

God has always been God. He is God. He will always be God. But when He saw how hopeless mankind was, the Almighty God sent His Son to become man.

Think of the humility it took for Christ to leave His splendor, glory, and majesty and live in a human body. He didn't *have* to allow Himself to be beaten with a whip. He didn't *have* to die for the sins of the world. But to reach us where we are, and because of His love for us, He did it.

What does it take to be humble? Should we be like the man who got a medal for his humility—and later the people who presented it made him give it back because he wanted to wear it all the time?

True biblical humility is the opposite of the popular world view of humility—showing how great you are by acting humble. The world view is rooted in pride and man's attempts to be like God. Though the scribes and Pharisees of Jesus' day knew much of the truth, they were proud. Their actions—prayer and fasting—were biblical. But their reasons were wrong. According to Jesus, they prayed to be seen by other men. And when they fasted, they made it blatant so they would earn spiritual points with their friends.

Jesus spoke against this false humility, this pride. And the Old Testament Book of Proverbs is so full of references to this sin it takes a long time to track them all down.

Jesus Didn't Need an Appointment Book

This false humility and pride kept me from coming to Christ for many years. When I was in high school in Baton Rouge, La. I was president of the Junior Rotarians, the Thespian (drama) Society, and of the East Baton Rouge Parish Youth Council, made up of heads of all the student governments in the area.

All these activities were supposed to help people and help the community, which is a wonderful thing for a person to do, right? But my attitude was wrong. It wasn't the good of the people of the community that motivated me. It was the ego of one Sammy Tippit. I was proud. I wanted people to know how good I was. God couldn't be pleased with such a life; and though I often heard He was interested in me, I didn't see any need for Him in my crowded life.

I thought I was a good person. And I've found that as I've shared my faith with people from all kinds of jobs and from all social and economic levels, more often than not, the excuse I hear when they reject my witness is, "But I'm a good person."

This "goodness" is contrary to the Word of God. People are not good. People without God are lost.

It makes me wonder, if people are so good, why are our jails overflowing and our court dockets jammed? Why is the divorce rate so high? Why do people distrust each other? The only way people can become true followers of Jesus is to see that their own "goodness" is nothing. We can do nothing in ourselves to please God. Paul wrote, "I know that nothing good dwells in me" (Romans 7:18).

This is not to say that God doesn't use and bless anybody's talents. He does. But if we depend on ourselves alone to be effective for Him or to make us like Him, we're in trouble. The Bible says, "Whoever exalts himself shall be humbled; and whoever humbles himself shall be exalted" (Matthew 23:12). In other words, if we come before God feeling that we've really got something to offer and with the attitude that we're going to do great things for Him, we're going to be humbled whether we want to be or not.

But if we say, "God, in myself I can do nothing," He will use the abilities He gave us in wonderful ways. The key is total dependence, absolute dependence, on God. This is the example of Jesus Himself. Jesus said, "When you lift up the Son of Man, then you will know that I am He, and I do nothing on My own initiative, but I speak these things as the Father taught Me" (John 8:28). (See also John 14:10.)

The work of God is not to be done in our own strength, but rather the way Jesus did it, through depending on the Father.

Billy G. and Me!

When I was 16—a couple years before I became a Christian—I was named the outstanding youth speaker in North America in competition at the United Nations international oratorical contest. I was one of only 30 students from Louisiana to travel to New York City to study with students from all over the United States and Canada at the UN. When I returned to Baton Rouge, I'll tell you, I thought I had the world by the tail. I was really *it*.

The reputation I earned from this experience was the key to my landing the prestige offices in school groups I mentioned earlier. I thought that I didn't need any help in my life. But the day came when I heard the right message from the right speaker at the right time and the Holy Spirit began to work in my heart. After I became a Christian, I felt God calling me to preach. I was so excited about my new relationship with Him and with my new faith that I wanted to share my faith with everybody. And what better way than through my speaking ability?

Here I was, just out of high school, on my way to college, a new Christian, surrendering to God's call to preach. With my superb background in public speaking and my enthusiasm, I thought I might be the next Billy Graham! Surely God would use my life, with all I had to offer.

I spoke everywhere—at missions, rest homes, churches, youth meetings, rallies, crusades—you name it. I knew how to gesture, how to use my voice inflections, when to shout, when to whisper, when to be funny, when to slam home the point with an illustration. I thought I was really something.

Trouble was, God wasn't using me.

No one was coming to know Jesus. Lives weren't changed. Christians weren't growing closer to Christ or deeper in their commitment. Oh, I was gaining a following of people who enjoyed a flashy sermon. And people would respond with laughing or crying or "amen"-ing or with compliments. But there was no fruitfulness in my life and I didn't know why—till one day I read a short chapter in a small book whose title I don't even remember.

The book said that dependence on our own abilities keeps us from being a successful worker for God. Despite what we might seem to accomplish on the outside, very little gets accomplished on the inside. God showed me I had been doing everything on my own initiative. I cried as I realized that the puzzling obstacle to God's blessing on my ministry had been me. I hadn't been a helper of God's; I'd been a roadblock. When I repented and asked God's forgiveness, He began to bless me. When my old self was out of the way, He worked in ways that by myself I never could have.

The next weekend I was scheduled to speak in a small church in southern Louisiana. I had meetings Friday and Saturday nights and Sunday morning and night. Only about 20 people came Friday night, but for the first time I began to speak without depending on my own ability or power but rather surrendering to what the Spirit of God wanted to do through me. Almost every person there made a decision either for salvation or rededication to Christ. Next night the church was jammed with a record crowd.

Sunday morning's attendance broke Saturday night's record, and Sunday night I couldn't even find a parking place. God had worked in a dramatic way, and I wouldn't take one bit of credit. I had started with much larger crowds on my own power and saw no results. Now here, with a tiny beginning, were dozens of people coming to Christ, deciding to become preachers and evangelists and other types of full-time Christian workers. Many people who are preaching the Gospel of Jesus Christ today were converted at that four-meeting crusade in Louisiana.

Jesus promised His followers, "I am the Vine, you are the branches; he who abides in Me, and I in him, he bears much fruit; for apart from Me you can do nothing" (John 15:5). That truth was driven home to me quite effectively, but I still had more to learn about humility.

The Servant Spirit

Jesus said, "The greatest among you shall be your servant" (Matthew 23:11). Remember when Jesus washed the disciples' feet? (John 13:3-11) Think of the One we are talking about here: the God of splendor, the God-Man, taking on Himself the servant spirit to commit such an act of humility! It was His example to us. A proud person will not act as a servant, but a truly humble person will.

When our street ministry was headquartered in Chicago a few years ago, we had 13 full-time workers, none of whom, it seemed, liked to do dirty work—including me. We all wanted to lead the nightly Bible studies that saw gang members, runaways, prostitutes, and drug addicts receive Jesus. And we all loved the excitement of witnessing on the street with its danger and often miraculous results.

But scrubbing the floors—which had to be done daily because we had a lot of foot traffic in the house—was nobody's favorite job, to say the least. We knew it was an important part of our witness to maintain a neat and orderly place, but it was gripe-and-complain time whenever the job came due. It got to be a serious problem, and God even quit blessing our ministry. We didn't know what had happened. Things had been so big and exciting and fun and dramatic. Now suddenly, nothing. "Apart from Me you can do nothing."

We finally decided that God was trying to tell us something: that no one had a servant spirit. We agreed in prayer that the next time it came our turn to scrub the floors, we'd consider it an opportunity to love and serve Jesus.

It worked. Often you could hear the floor scrubber singing, "O How I Love Jesus" and praising the Lord. It electrified the atmosphere, and a revival took place in our ministry. God began blessing our work again.

The common characteristic among great men of God is humility. God calls a humble person great. And not many were humble—or great—at first. They were proud and frail, but their humility grew with their spiritual maturity.

The Bible teaches us that there was not a greater prophet to arise in all of Israel than Moses. Yet Moses is called the *"servant"* of the Lord (Deuteronomy 34:5; Joshua 1:1; Numbers 12:7). He was a great man of God, yet he was still a servant.

If you want to be great in the kingdom of God, take the attitude of a servant. Why are so many churches full of people who want to be on the front lines, doing the glamorous, spectacular jobs, but so few who want to work behind the scenes in menial tasks? Paul, who was one of the greatest men of God in the New Testament, continually referred to himself as a bond servant of the one and only Lord Jesus.

Joshua is also referred to as a servant (Exodus 33:11). Yet God was preparing him to be the leader of the nation of Israel. If you want God to use your life, you'll have to learn what the great men of the Bible had to learn: how to be a humble servant.

Don't take my word for it. Take Jesus' word. "You know that the rulers of the Gentiles lord [their power] over them, and their great men exercise authority over them. It is not so among you, but whoever wishes to become great among you shall be your servant, and whoever wishes to be first among you shall become your slave; just as the Son of Man did not come to be served, but to serve, and to give His life a ransom for many" (Matthew 20:25-28).

The Grateful Spirit

I still had more to learn about humility. Fortunately, God had patience with me. Though I had learned total dependence on God for my preaching, I did not see my fault in the area of not having a servant spirit. I was the leader; I had always been a leader; my leadership ability was a gift. I had even dedicated it to God. That's why I was puzzled when my old style of you-do-this-and-you-do-that-and-we'll-all-fall-in-and-get-it-done didn't work now. I had trouble with my staff members. Interpersonal relationships became strained. Here was a ministry otherwise blessed of God—people coming to Christ —yet there was trouble in the ranks.

It was when I read "whoever wishes to be first

among you shall become your slave" that it washed over me. Though Christ had come into my life and had led me in many important areas, I was still trying to be a leader in the way of the world and not in God's way. The way of the world is to take command and start barking orders. Jesus' way is to become a servant. When God opened my eyes to this, it broke my heart. I loved my co-workers, but I'm sure they didn't sense it. I had been trying to be a leader simply by exercising my authority. I had to repent and ask their forgiveness. When that took place, a strange thing happened.

I realized that I had never been grateful for what people had done in our ministry. I had been so hung up on the world's style of heavy-handed leadership that my co-workers never did anything more than I expected. But now, with a servant spirit, working with our people rather than standing over them, I found myself grateful for everything they contributed to the work.

Paul wrote of people who are proud: "For even though they knew God, they did not honor Him as God, or give thanks; but they became futile in their speculations, and their foolish hearts were darkened. Professing to be wise, they became fools" (Romans 1:21-22).

Sin Consciousness

The whole purpose of Jesus' coming to earth was to seek and to save the lost. When He came into the presence of sin, He thought of it in relation to His ultimate assignment. He would take the world's sins on Himself on the cross so that you and I might become perfect in God's eyes. A person who is truly humble is a person who is very sensitive to sin.

Read Isaiah 6:1-5, and see what happened when a great prophet came into the presence of the glory of God. He saw himself as unclean, unworthy, sinful. The first thing he did when he saw God's glory was to cry out in shame. Don't think that just because you don't drink or do dope or act ugly that you're a together person. The closer you get to Christ, the more unworthy you'll see yourself.

Paul, one of the greatest apostles, called himself the chief sinner (1 Timothy 1:15). I believe biblical humility is rooted in sensitivity to sin. Just as you can't see some people's freckles except under a bright light, our blemishes become more apparent in the light of God's truth, when we're close to Jesus, the Light of the World.

One Warning

Be careful not to fake humility just to impress someone. Humility is a characteristic of Jesus and one we should seek, but only for the purpose of being like Christ. Remember that the scribes and Pharisees were motivated by pride to look humble. A person seen trying hard to appear humble is hardly humble at all. Humility is an attitude of the heart, not an outward appearance.

Humble yourself truly before God by depending on Him completely, taking a servant spirit, and you'll find yourself with a heightened awareness of sin.

3
Love that Doesn't Quit

"Let me ask you something," I said to the young Communist. "Do you love the President of the United States?"

The young man, one of the elite Communist young people who had come to East Berlin for the Communist Youth World Festival, was trying to convince me that Communists loved everyone.

He frowned at my question. "Of course not! Are you kidding? He's a _ _ _ _ _ _ _ capitalist!"

"That's the difference between Christianity and Communism," I said. "As a Communist, you love those who love you. As a Christian, I can love any man because God's grace is that great."

Our love for each other sets us Christians apart from others like the Communist young man. The non-Christian world can judge us—and our faith—only by what it sees on the outside. And what it can see most quickly and clearly is whether we really love one another.

Think that's my idea? A Sammy Tippit-ism? If it

is, run it through your own screening process, and take it or leave it. But this point really came from Jesus Himself. (I try to base all my counsel on His Word. It will not fail or ever pass away.)

Jesus said, "A new commandment I give to you, that you love one another, even as I have loved you, that you also love one another. By this all men will know that you are My disciples" (John 13:34-35).

Christian love ought to be revolutionary, because we have a source of love that allows us to love in a way that no others in the world can love. I always thought that 1 John 4:16-17 dealt with personal victory over sin till I studied it carefully. Read it:

"And we have come to know and have believed the love which God has for us. God is love, and the one who abides in love abides in God, and God abides in him. By this, love is perfected with us, that we may have confidence in the day of judgment, because as He is, so also are we in this world."

The whole point of discipleship is becoming like Jesus Christ. If He is our example, we should do as He did. We are to love others as Jesus does. He is the God of love.

At the Communist World Fest, we were expecting to be the only 3 Christians among 100,000 elite Communist young people from all over the world. They were there to learn how to evangelize the whole world for Communism. We were there to evangelize the world for Jesus. We tried many different tactics; but one of the most effective, we found, was to start preaching and keep preaching as a crowd gathered. We were afraid of being arrested, but the whole world was watching and the Communist authorities used us as a token example that they happily allowed freedom of speech.

One day, when I had finished preaching, a young man cornered me. "I've got you, I've finally got you," he said.

"What do you mean, you've got me?"

"I've caught you. There's another Christian preacher here from the Netherlands, and he's saying that after a person receives Christ, he can turn his back on Christ and lose his salvation. That doesn't sound like what you were saying!"

"That's right," I said. "I'm convinced that once a person has been saved, he's always saved." But I was so excited to find someone else at the World Fest who was preaching the Gospel that I asked the man to take me to the Dutchman.

When we were introduced, I asked him if he were preaching the Gospel. He said he was. I asked him if he were preaching that a person could lose his salvation under certain circumstances. He said he was. And while my young critic looked on dumbfounded, we embraced and praised the Lord for each other.

"What are you doing?" demanded the onlooker. "I thought you disagreed!"

"We do," I said. "But the fact that this man does not agree does not make us any less brothers in Christ."

The greatest lesson either of us taught that day was a lesson of love for each other. Of course, I would be careful about agreeing with someone who preached a false or heretical doctrine; and I admit that this preacher and I disagree on an important issue. But we both believe that Jesus is the Christ, the Son of the living God, and that by believing, people can have life through His name. That makes us brothers, and we love each other.

Characteristics of Jesus' Love

One of the first qualities we discover of Jesus' love is that He loved the hordes of people that followed Him around. When Jesus saw a certain crowd, He "felt compassion for them, and healed their sick. And when it was evening, the disciples came to Him, saying, 'The place is desolate, and the time is already past; so send the multitudes away, that they may go to the villages and buy food for themselves.' But Jesus said to them, 'They do not need to go away; you give them something to eat!' " (Matthew 14:14-16)

The disciples were ready to dump the crowd. In trying to appear concerned for the welfare of the 5,000 men and their women and children, they found an excuse to try to send them away.

But Jesus would have none of their unconcern. He felt compassion toward these people and in effect told His disciples that they should love the people the same way He loved the disciples. He told Peter three times that if Peter loved Him, he should feed His "sheep" (John 21:15).

Jesus fed the crowd that followed Him. Do we do the same? Or do we often say to those who need Christ but are different from us, "Uh—why don't you try that other church down the street"—and slam the door in their faces.

Some say, "I love Jesus and I want to follow Him, but I'm into discipling one person at a time, pouring my life into him." Others say, "We're locked into a small-group situation." Satan has snowed the Christian church on this issue. We can't ignore the fact that Jesus loved the multitudes. It's simple. If we are to be like Jesus, then we, like Him, must also reach out to the masses of the unchurched.

A Christian friend and I visited the Soviet Union a few years ago and headed straight for the University of Leningrad where we found students who understood English and who were hungry for the Gospel. One young man told us that he'd been taught all his life that there was no God. Yet he had doubted this teaching and had prayed, "God, if there is a God, reveal Yourself to me." He told us that he believed God had revealed Himself to him through our witness and asked if we had any more of the tracts he had seen us passing out. We gave him a bunch, and he began circulating them. Before long, a crowd of students appeared, curious about what we had to say.

After about 45 minutes of bold preaching, my friend and I were arrested by six KGB agents who hustled us off for eight and one-half hours of questioning. We were confined to a room and threatened with jail before we were finally deported to Helsinki, Finland. But we were able to share Christ with some of the agents, and what they told us about our crime was an eye-opener.

They said they believed that the Christian church would be gone by the year 2000. We knew it was not against the law to go to church in the Soviet Union because we had visited a big church the night before and saw many people there—mostly old people because the young people have gone "underground."

"We believe," the Soviets told us, "that those who go to church are sick people; but if they want to be sick, we give them that right. But if someone leaves that church and tries to spread his sickness, he has committed a crime against the people of the Soviet Union."

That's what we had done, they said. "By spreading your Word, you have spread a disease."

I learned a great lesson from that experience. God showed me that Satan is not so concerned if we simply go to church and hold our nice little worship services. What makes him angry is when we go out and try to feed the multitudes. Satan has trapped the American church, not through government regulations and laws, as in the Soviet Union, but through apathy.

God wants His message to go to all. (See Mark 3:14.) They may not believe; but again, if we are to be like Jesus, our goal should be to give the entire world an opportunity to receive Him.

I've heard people say that they don't want to go to church with a bunch of hypocrites (in other words, with those who aren't as spiritual as they are). Jesus spent time not only with those who loved Him, but with cheating tax collectors as well; and we must do the same. It's impossible to be a loner and be like Jesus. Spend time with peers, with older people; disciple a friend. Fellowship, study, learn of Jesus together. Your love for each other will grow. Nothing can duplicate the heavenly love believers have for each other, in spite of petty problems and personality differences.

Because we are different, we have to learn this love. It may not come naturally. Peter was a talker, emotional, impulsive, the first to pledge his allegiance to the Master and the first to deny Him when hard times came. John was temperamental. Thomas was a doubting intellectual. Matthew was a money man. Jesus called men who were not originally superspiritual to be His disciples.

Anyone can love someone who is just like himself. It's a form of self-love. But love someone in spite of personality conflicts, and let the love of Jesus override your differences, and you will truly love your brothers and sisters the way Christ loves them.

I've had to learn this difficult lesson because of my personality. When I'm preaching or witnessing, I'm outgoing. But when I meet people informally, I'm quiet and reserved. So I often get branded as being stuck-up or aloof. The problem is probably more one of shyness than anything else. I've had to learn to love people who have misjudged me, and I've had to learn to work on making a better impression.

What sets Christian love apart is that Christians should have the capacity to love even those with whom they disagree. Christ loved sinners. This is the toughest part of learning this kind of love. Too often we get in our corners with our spiritual boxing gloves ready, and want to knock off another Christian because he holds an opposing view of something. I don't believe in compromising on views I feel God has given me from Scripture, but neither do I have to duke it out with a brother.

Another characteristic of the love of Jesus is that He not only talked love, but His actions also proved He felt compassion for others. "We know love by this, that He laid down His life for us; and we ought to lay down our lives for the brethren. But whoever has the world's goods, and beholds his brother in need and closes his heart against him, how does the love of God abide in him? Little children, let us not love with word or with tongue, but in deed and truth" (1 John 3:16-18).

A lot of Christians run around saying "God bless you Jesus loves you and I do too," but don't turn their halfhearted words into concrete expressions of concern. In the Chicago ghetto, we ran into dozens of people every day who needed the basics of survival. Our resources were completely inadequate for the size of the need.

We prayed that God would find a way we could help. One day a bakery truck pulled up in front of our place. The driver told us that his boss wanted to donate baked goods to our ministry. We found ourselves with cakes, pies, doughnuts, bread, and rolls that had to be stacked in my office for lack of other space.

It was so much more than even our small staff could use that God soon impressed on us that the food was His answer to prayer. We began looking for people in need and found many who hadn't eaten all day. We ministered to their bodies, and then we ministered to their souls. Many evangelicals are afraid to love in this way because they think it smacks of social gospel. It's not. It's part of becoming like Jesus.

Of course, when you begin to love through your actions you have to prayerfully determine just what the need is. I've had winos ask me for money. They were poor, and I had money, but the money would have been the worst thing for them for an obvious reason. I asked them what they wanted it for and they always answered, "for some food." So I began carrying a sack lunch with me on the streets to give to anyone who asked for food.

Suppose I've been asked to help a person meet a financial need, say a Christian brother who can't pay the rent. Perhaps the money is just what he needs now, but maybe his need is just a symptom of a bigger need. Maybe what he really needs is financial and spiritual counseling to teach him how to make a budget. There are many ways you can help people.

Problem Relationships

Relationships with a Christian brother or sister can be broken in two ways: through something you have said or done (or haven't done) or through a bad attitude you have developed. Let's deal with the easy one, bad attitude, first.

If you don't like someone or aren't comfortable around him, my advice is *not* to go to him and confess your hang-up. That may sound noble at first, but imagine someone coming to you and saying, "Friend, I can't stand you. I'm sorry. I just wanted to get that off my chest."

A better solution is to give your bad attitude to God first. Tell Him you know you are wrong to have bad feelings toward a fellow Christian and pray that He will heal you. The person will probably not change overnight, but you may. You will learn things about yourself and you will find yourself going out of your way to be nice to that person. It's amazing what God does in us.

Now, for the tougher problem. When a rift has been caused by your having done or said something (or not done something), there is only one solution. You must go to the person and make it right. Admit your fault, and expect nothing in return. Generally, both parties are partially wrong, but the other person's guilt is none of your concern. Admit your guilt and ask forgiveness. Go in humility, not with pride that says you're the more spiritual of the two. Withdraw your damaging comments from anyone who might have heard them, or make right whatever other wrong you may have committed.

That's the only way to repair a broken relationship and retain communion with God. Of course, you must also deal with God privately, asking His forgiveness, grace, and help.

Get Your Tongue Down to Size

Gossip is one of the most dangerous faults in the church. Gossip can be true, you know, and still be wrong. Let's define gossip as news that harms the teller, the hearer, and the one being talked about. For instance, say someone is in trouble. You tell a friend (who is not part of the solution), and that friend thinks less of you because you said it and less of the person in trouble. All three of you have been cheapened.

There are times, of course, when painful news must be shared—but those times should be carefully judged by the extent to which the hearer can help. If the hearer can't help, there's no reason to mention it.

I've always enjoyed the joke about the gossip who went forward in a service and told the pastor, "I've been convicted about my gossiping and I want to lay my tongue on the altar."

"I'm sorry," the pastor replied, "but our altar is only 20 feet long!"

What about relationships that are broken for reasons that you can't understand? That's the time to pray, with the psalmist, "Search me, O God, and know my heart.... See if there be any hurtful way in me" (Psalm 139:23). Believe me, it works. Once, when I was in college, we were asked to go off by ourselves to "get right with God."

We were to confess all known sin, write it down, and ask God to cleanse us. Then we were to ask His Holy Spirit to let us know of those sins we couldn't think of or those things we'd never thought of as sin before. I had to go back for more paper!

Another good exercise is to go to someone you trust or even to the person you have a problem with and ask him if he is aware of anything in your life that isn't right and about which you need help. Your action might surprise him, but it might do wonders for you. It's always easy to see someone else's faults, but it's hard to see your own. Sometimes I think God allows you to see a fault in someone else's life so you can be careful of that same tendency yourself. So instead of spreading gossip about it, you should examine yourself and pray for God to strengthen you against the same temptation.

Discipline

Ouch, you were afraid we'd come to this, right? Love always brings discipline. The Lord Himself says: "Those whom I love, I reprove and discipline; be zealous therefore, and repent" (Revelation 3:19).

The church often ignores situations where discipline should be lovingly administered. Emphasis on the *lovingly* is necessary. Discipline is designed to help, not hurt, a guilty party. When an older brother or sister in Christ or a parent tries to correct you, don't become defensive, upset, angry, or bitter.

Understand that the person loves you. The world says that those who try to correct us don't love us. But the Bible says we should discipline those we love (Luke 17:3).

Some people bomb out of Christianity because they were disappointed in certain Christians they knew. They didn't know Christianity would be like this, or that Christians would do such things. We can't escape the fact that we're human. We're not perfect, but we have access to the great Problem-Solver and to an unlimited, unconditional Love Source that allows us to show supernatural compassion to the world and to our own brothers and sisters.

God loved us first (1 John 4:19). He beat us to it. He doesn't love us because we love Him. It's the other way around. Love produces faith and hope and expects the best in people. Love endures all, according to 1 Corinthians 13:7. What an example for us and to the world!

Enduring love. That's the love of God. Read Philippians 1:6 right now, and praise God for sticking with you: "For I am confident of this very thing, that He who began a good work in you will perfect it till the day of Christ Jesus."

PRAYER

4
Becoming like Jesus—in Prayer

If you could ask Jesus for one specific thing only, what would you want?

Maybe you'd ask Him to get you a date with the best-looking guy or girl in the school. Or maybe you'd ask for a new stereo, a new set of tires, or some electronic game.

Instead of being funny or cute, you might get pretty spiritual in your thinking. Instead of tires, a stereo, or whatever, you might ask Him to help someone or really change your life in some way.

The disciples had many chances to ask Jesus for things. But one particular thing they asked for was to teach them to pray (Luke 11:1-4).

Jesus told them: "When you pray, you are not to be as the hypocrites, for they love to stand and pray in the synagogues and on the street corners in order to be seen by men. Truly I say to you, they have their reward in full. But you, when you pray, go into your inner room, and when you have shut your door, pray to your Father who is in secret, and your

Father who sees in secret will repay you.

"And when you are praying, do not use meaningless repetition, as the Gentiles do, for they suppose that they will be heard for their many words. Therefore do not be like them; for your Father knows what you need before you ask Him.

"Pray, then, in this way:
'Our Father who art in heaven,
hallowed be Thy name.
Thy kingdom come.
Thy will be done,
on earth as it is in heaven.
Give us this day our daily bread.
And forgive us our debts, as we also have forgiven our debtors.
And do not lead us into temptation, but deliver us from evil. For Thine is the kingdom, and the power, and the glory, forever. Amen' " (Matthew 6:5-13).

One thing Christianity needs badly is a great army of children, young people, and adults who will pray. Miracles can take place in our lives if we learn to pray.

How Not to Pray

Jesus began answering the disciples' question by telling them how *not* to pray. We shouldn't be public about it, He said. We have already discussed the characteristic of humility. How humble can we be if we are praying because we want our egos pumped up?

Prayer is not meant to be a glamorous task that wins pats on the back for the person praying. Now this doesn't mean that we should never pray in church or at a meal or with other Christians in any setting. The principle here is motive.

We live in a superstar age where people look for the exciting and the spectacular. But Jesus says the rewards of secret prayer are eternal and that we shouldn't pray to impress others.

He also says that we should not use vain repetition. No doubt you've heard people say the same thing over and over in their prayers. It's something to guard against, according to this teaching. If we don't constantly think about the words and their meanings, the Lord's Prayer itself could become a vain repetition.

Our Father Who Art in Heaven

Jesus begins with the word *our*. We can't enjoy the benefits of any of the principles taught by this prayer unless we know beyond doubt that God is *our* Father.

If you aren't a Christian, you can't pray, "our Father." And the devil will have a heyday with you if you are a Christian who doubts your salvation. If you can't answer positively to the following question, you'll never be able to pray effectively: If you died right now, are you absolutely sure you'd go to heaven?

If you can't answer *yes*, either you've never become a Christian or you doubt your salvation. There's one answer to both problems. Make sure. Here's how:

Realize that you can never work your way into heaven. Too many people think that God is everybody's Father. They say that everyone is a child of

God. But the Bible says otherwise: "For you are the children of your father the devil, and you love to do the evil things he does" (John 8:44, LB).

Paul says that our nature is sinful and that we all qualify as sinners and not as sons of God (Romans 3:23). We don't like to hear that. I like to think I'm good and can do no wrong, but once I admit that the Bible is right about me, I can see why Jesus died for my sins. The only way to become a child of God is to receive Jesus Christ as Lord and Saviour of our lives.

Then, trust Him and not your feelings. When Christ saves you, the transaction is complete. It doesn't make any difference whether or not you feel saved. If you've prayed the prayer and meant it, you're saved.

Hallowed Be Thy Name

When we praise the name of God, we worship Him because of His character—for who He is and what He has done. There should be an element of praise and worship of God in every prayer we say. Praising Him is one of the most beautiful growth experiences a disciple can have.

Hallowed means that His name is to be revered, adored, honored, respected. Among the Jews, a person's name signified character. Paul's name was changed from Saul after his character went through a radical change at the time of his conversion to Christ.

In my own prayer time I have begun something new that you might want to try. I sing hymns and Scripture songs and choruses to God and find it a real joy. (That's something, when you consider what a terrible singer I am.)

People who don't know how to praise the Lord miss out on the joy of God. Pick out one of His qualities, and praise Him for it. Worship Him because He is love, or because He is all-powerful, or because He is the Creator.

Thy Kingdom Come. Thy Will Be Done, On Earth as It Is in Heaven

Much of our praying should be devoted to determining what God's will is for situations in our lives.

Now, how do we know God's will? In some instances His Word is crystal clear, with such phrases as, "The will of God concerning you is. . . ." Check a good concordance and see if you can find what the will of God is in areas where you've been having problems. It will save some needless praying about whether you should or should not do certain things.

But the specific will of God in *some* situations is not spelled out word-for-word in Scripture, however. In such cases, I normally use a three-part test: (1) Do I feel an inner peace about a future course of action I could take? (2) Does something in Scripture give me a hint about what I should do? (3) Is something happening in my life that will help me make a decision?

If I get what I think is a leading from the Lord, I first decide whether I feel an inner peace about it. Since God is the God of peace and not of confusion, if I feel upset, troubled, and confused, the leading can't be of God.

Then I check my feeling against what I know from Scripture to make sure it doesn't contradict any biblical principles, for God never contradicts Himself. Finally something may happen in my life, such as a confirming word from a trusted friend or relative. Or an event will show me that what I have been led to as a solution is actually valid.

The Old Testament Judge Gideon was called by God to free the Israelites from their oppressors. But Gideon doubted God really chose him. So he asked for a sign from heaven. God directed him to put lamb's meat and a loaf of bread out on a rock. Suddenly, as Gideon watched, the meat and bread burst into flames—touched by an angel. Gideon immediately praised God and went on his mission (Judges 6:11-27). God won't offer us smoked lamb every time He wants us to do something, but His Holy Spirit will often give us signs that we are—or aren't—on the right track.

This idea makes Bible study and prayer go together, doesn't it? You must know God's Word if you want His heavenly will to be done on earth.

There are promises in Scripture for all kinds of situations and circumstances. For instance, when I go to preach somewhere, the first thing I do is pray with someone and claim the promise that where two or three are gathered in the name of Jesus that He will be there too. It is His will already accomplished in heaven, and I want it done on earth. It's also His will that none should perish.

We don't see God more active in our Sunday School classes and youth groups and churches because many of us haven't *tried* to discover His will. Much of our prayer should be simply claiming the promises of God.

Give Us This Day Our Daily Bread

We should pray every day.

One of the great needs in any Christian's life is daily prayer. I have to pray every day to stay in shape spiritually. I can't get along without it. It's a matter of discipline. If you want to become a more mature Christian, you must be consistent in this area.

The youth group in one church I preached in got all excited about Jesus. They were going to tear up their town for God. A year later when I came back they were tired, out of it, bored, defeated. What happened? I asked.

"We don't know," they mumbled.

"How many of you spent at least 15 minutes a day in prayer and Bible reading over the last year?" I asked. Not one raised a hand.

What would you say if I said I was going to eat only once a week, on Sunday? I might eat both morning and evening, but only on Sunday? You'd say, "You'll be one skinny guy!" But don't we often do that in our prayer lives? We say, "Lord, I want to be strong for You," but then we only eat the Bread of Life one day a week.

I know that the pray-in-the-morning business has some of you reeling already. I know. I'm lousy in the morning too. I'm so bad that my wife has to get up 30 minutes earlier than I do so she can have her own devotions in peace. If I kneel by the bed to pray or sit at a table or with a friend, I'll likely fall asleep a few minutes into the prayer. I've had friends pray, "Lord, give me the peace You just gave ol' Sam!"

So, I get off in a room by myself and I pace. That gets the circulation going, and I can concentrate as I talk to God and sing praises to Him.

Forgive Us Our Debts

Praise should be a major part of our prayer lives. But praise by someone unholy is an abomination to God. God won't honor the prayer of an unconfessed sinner. If you wonder why God doesn't answer a prayer, ask Him to let you know of an unconfessed sin in your life. Then confess it. His forgiveness is freely given, and we need it to pray effectively.

As We Also Have Forgiven Our Debtors

We owe God a greater debt for the forgiveness of our sins than anyone could ever owe us. Jesus died on the cross for our sins. We were the beneficiaries of this great forgiveness, love, and mercy. Our prayers don't count till we show a fraction of that love, by forgiving others for what they did to us.

I once went into a nightclub in Chicago and began talking to people about God. The owner asked me what I was up to so I began sharing my faith with him. He was interested and allowed me to come back and even preach in his place during breaks in the music. After several months of this, he seemed that he wanted to receive Christ as his Saviour.

As we walked on a Lake Michigan beach one day he told me that one thing was keeping him from receiving Christ. "Sammy," he said, "I am into the mob for a lot of money, and if I become a Christian and walk out on them now, they'll kill me."

I asked him how much he owed. He told me.

"I have that much money," I said eagerly. "My wife and I have been saving for months, ever since we found out she was pregnant. I'd be happy to give you that money if it meant that you would be free of the mob and could receive Jesus. It would be a small price for the salvation of your soul."

So, the next day he took the money and prayed in tears to receive Christ. We were overjoyed, and I set an appointment with him the next day to begin a discipleship program. But the next day he was nowhere to be found. I went to the nightclub and there I learned I had been taken. He was one of the biggest cons going, and he had ripped me off. He wasn't interested in receiving Christ, but he had an interest in whatever money I had.

I could have been bitter at him and at God, but I refused bitterness and forgave him because God had forgiven me for much more than that. And God honored that. He replaced the money by leading both the doctor and the hospital to charge much less than normal for my son's delivery, and friends gave us large amounts of money in small gifts. When we're obedient to the Lord, He blesses and meets our needs.

And Lead Us Not into Temptation But Deliver Us from Evil

The principle here is obedience to God. We become powerful in prayer as we become obedient to God. I wish I could say that every time I prayed, God did something. But I knew many times before I went to prayer that I was not meeting His requirements. He demands that we abide in Him and that His words abide in us (John 15:7); then we can ask what we will and it will be done.

Read Proverbs 6:16-19, and you will see what God hates. One thing He hates is feet that run to evil. We are to flee evil. Flee whatever tries to drag you down. If we hang around temptation and allow sin a foothold, our prayer lives will be ruined.

That doesn't necessarily mean we should jump into our running shoes as soon as we see a non-Christian. (We can't witness to the unsaved without meeting them, right?) But we shouldn't let our thoughts be constantly dragged down to the level of the world's, with its emphasis on violence, bed partners, and getting ahead of the other guy.

Our whole continent is developing a desire for evil. You can see it in the commercials on TV, in the magazines we read, just everywhere. But the Christian is to flee the pressure to conform to what the world does.

For Thine Is the Kindgom and the Power and the Glory Forever. Amen.

One day an associate of mine gave me $20 and said that a man from the church had given him twice that to split with me because the Lord told him we would have a need for it. Neither of us could think of a specific need for it, so we decided to pray about it.

The Lord led us to use the money to spend the

whole day in a hotel room praying about our upcoming trip to the Communist Youth World Festival.

We felt God was telling us that He would break the power of Communism and atheism in the lives of many at the Fest. And then we read: "God will shed His own glorious light on you. He will heal you; your godliness will lead you forward, and goodness will be a shield before you, and the glory of the Lord will protect you from behind" (Isaiah 58:8, LB).

Did you catch that? The glory of the Lord will protect us from behind! A few months later, the promise was proven. When the Communists tried to break up our meetings and drown out my preaching by shouting, we fell to our knees in prayer and a downpour of rain sent the troublemakers scattering. We ran for the shelter of an overhang where 2,000 other Communists listened to our message, uninterrupted for the rest of the evening.

By the last night of the Fest, 200 Communists had received Jesus and began to march with us in His name. But when Communist leaders sent 1,000 agitators to break us up, it looked as if there were 1,200 Christians marching! All over the square, tens of thousands of people shouted, "Here come the Christians!"

I couldn't begin to estimate the crowd that heard our message that night. Jesus was the talk of the Fest, which had been called to evangelize the world for atheistic Communism.

We need people who will become like Jesus in their prayer lives. Ask Jesus to teach you to pray.

HIS WORD

5
What's the Good Word?

The blizzard was intense. All traffic had stopped. Fifteen people were trapped in a Howard Johnson's restaurant in a lonely corner of the Midwest.

Then the phone went dead.

For two days no one could call in, and no one could talk to anyone on the outside. Those 15 people could hear only the whistling of the storm. They wondered if and when they would be discovered.

Can you imagine what it would be like to be cut off from God—not just for two days, but for all our lives? What if He had no way of reaching us with the news of salvation? What if we didn't have the option of receiving eternal life?

But we don't have that problem.

God has chosen to reach us—to speak to us—through His Son. Jesus Christ is the living Word of God. And the Bible is God's written Word. To become like Jesus, we just get to know and follow the Word of God.

The Bible puts it this way: "In the past God spoke to our forefathers through the prophets at many times and in various ways, but in these last days He has spoken to us by His Son, whom He appointed heir of all things, and through whom He made the universe" (Hebrews 1:1-2, NIV).

And the Bible also says, "In the beginning was the Word, and the Word was with God, and the Word was God" (John 1:1).

Think of the Bible as simply the written testimony of the living Jesus. We are to make the Bible a reality in our lives.

Scribes and Pharisees, "religious" men of Jesus' day, tried to trick Jesus and catch Him on a point of Scripture or doctrine. Jesus told them that even though they knew the Scriptures, just reading them doesn't bring eternal life (John 5:39).

If we search the Scriptures for any reason other than to know God more deeply and the life He wants for us, we have the wrong motive. Before we can deal with the Word of God, we have to see it in its proper light, as testifying to Jesus and the Christ-like life. Then, as we study and meditate on it, we will be taking the character of Jesus as a model for ourselves.

The Importance of the Word in Our Lives

For a look at what the disciple Peter thought of Scripture, read 2 Peter 1:16-21. Peter tells that he was an eyewitness to many of the events surrounding Jesus. Yet he goes on to say that he has an even more sure witness—the Scriptures and their prophecy of the events he described. The Word of

What's the Good Word? / 59

God can be more important than our own experience, even, in Peter's case, more important than being witness of the facts and words of Jesus.

Our experiences can tell us different things at different times. But the Word of God is always the same. Our actions should be based on the Word of God. For instance, experience may tell us if we take a little money from our parents without their knowing about it, they'll probably never realize it's gone. But the Bible says we should not steal. Jesus is the Way (John 14:6); and His Word, the Bible, is the Lamp that can keep our feet from slipping off the path into darkness. (Many cults are born because someone has stolen a verse out of context to explain a specific experience.)

Ways to Make the Word Come to Life For You

If you'll apply the following eight principles to your time with the Bible, the Holy Spirit will help you to grow in Christ.

- *Memorize the Word.*

"Thy Word I have treasured in my heart, that I may not sin against Thee" (Psalm 119:11). Memorizing Scripture can keep us from sin. It worked for Jesus. When He was tempted in the wilderness He quoted Scripture to the devil.

One of the first things I did when I became a Christian was to memorize Scripture. Even now, during crises, verses come to mind that I memorized during those first few months as a believer.

- *Meditate on the Word.*

There is a difference between meditating and memorizing. Meditating means thinking about something. "Finally, brethren, whatever is true, whatever is honorable, whatever is right, whatever is pure, whatever is lovely, whatever is of good repute, if there is any excellence and if anything worthy of praise, let your mind dwell on these things" (Philippians 4:8).

I jog five-eight miles a day and spend the whole time thinking about a Scripture verse or a story or a chapter. When I run with someone else, we share verses. It's really been a great way to keep fit and grow at the same time.

- *Read the Word.*

God's Word is His Letter to His people about His Son. If you are a Christian, with the right Bible study books and aids, you should find reading Scripture a very cleansing experience.

One problem you may have had is that you started reading the Bible in the wrong place. Some of you may start at the beginning and get lost in all the names and genealogies of Genesis. Then you may switch to the other end and get blown away by all the heavy imagery in Revelation. Why not start in the middle instead? Take a Psalm every day, read it over a few times, memorize a verse from it, and think about it all day. Then move on and do the same with Proverbs, and you'll have enough material to last you six months.

- *Hear the Word.*

"For since the messages from angels have always proved true and people have always been punished

What's the Good Word? / 61

for disobeying them, what makes us think that we can escape if we are indifferent to this great salvation announced by the Lord Himself?" (Hebrews 2:2-3, LB)

The Word is the testimony of Jesus; and Jesus is the Author of faith; so every time we hear it preached or taught, we should be open to Him. If you want to be a man or woman of faith, listen to sermons and lessons and messages and Bible studies. Hear the Word.

As an immature Christian I came to understand the importance of churchgoing while listening to a great preacher. I walked out in the middle of one of the meetings. I had to tell God that I didn't think I could ever have the kind of biblical faith he was talking about. God led me to listen to more good preaching and teaching till the Word became real to me and my faith came through hearing the Word of God.

- *Study the Word.*

The first three principles I listed should be done daily, the next at least once a week, and this one once a week too. There's a difference between studying and all the others. The Bible says that we should show ourselves to God as "approved" people, correctly understanding the Word of Truth (2 Timothy 2:15). How do we do that?

Take an area of Scripture or a topic, and use cross-references to see what the total teaching of the Bible is on it. For instance, if you read only Matthew 21:22 on prayer, which says everything you ask for will be given to you, you might think that you can ask God for a million dollars and you'll be sure to get it. But if you studied more of what the Bible teaches on prayer, you'd run across verses such as 1 John 5:14-17; Proverbs 2:3-5; and Jeremiah 33:3 which put certain conditions on prayer. We must pray in faith and in the will of God, we must try to act like Jesus, and His Word must live in us.

By studying, we see the whole picture more clearly. A good student needs a good concordance (a book that organizes Bible verses by the key words in them). It's worth the investment. Some people take passages totally out of context, and they wouldn't if they just used a good Bible study aid. The Word never contradicts itself. It always complements.

You might also want to shop for some topical Bible study books and Bible book studies.

- *Pray the Word*.

Sound strange? It isn't. There are many places in the Bible where Jesus, Paul, or someone else prays. These are good models for us, and they are also good for simply repeating as prayers. They make for good variety in our praying and add power as well. We have already discussed what we have to do to make our prayers effective. Think about how Jesus meets all the requirements. Therefore His prayers are perfect.

If there is a problem in your group or class, pray for unity the same way Christ prayed. If your friends or family have problems, pray, as Paul did for his friends, that those people will be strengthened. I've done this for my family. Find Scripture promises for your friends, your parents, your brothers, or your sisters, and make prayers out of those verses.

● *Do the Word*.

The Bible says, "But prove yourselves doers of the Word, and not merely hearers who delude themselves. For if anyone is a hearer of the Word and not a doer, he is like a man who looks at his natural face in a mirror; for once he has looked at himself and gone away, he has immediately forgotten what kind of person he was. But one who looks intently at the perfect law, the law of liberty, and abides by it, not having become a forgetful hearer but an effectual doer, this man shall be blessed in what he does" (James 1:22-25).

The Word is the testimony of Jesus. So if we keep hearing it but never do it, we'll never become like Jesus, the original Doer of His Word.

One of our problems, I think, is the freedom we enjoy. We take for granted all the things that Christians in Communist and other non-Christian countries risk their lives for. They don't have all the Christian literature that we have. Sometimes their only Bible is in their heads. They meet in secret and enjoy hard-earned fellowship. Sometimes I'm afraid it makes them better Christians because they are forced to concentrate on their faith. What do we do when we want to learn something about doctrine or love or whatever? We buy a book and study it for a few hours; then we think we know all we need to know.

A few years ago, when evangelicals began the trend of strengthening the family (a wonderful cause, of course), I studied the Scripture and came up with some real insight into being a better husband and father. The Lord really blessed the study; I came up with a long, pointed message on all aspects of the Christian family. I preached it till the

Lord told me very clearly that He had given me the message not to preach but to live. God would not let me be a hearer and a preacher till I had become a doer.

If we know the truth from Bible study, we must live it. The truth isn't for storage; it's for living. We have to make what we know a part of our daily lives. Suppose a person wants to be an auto mechanic but can't tell a carburetor from a hubcap (and so fouls everything up when he sticks his head under the hood). He goes to a trade school and learns about cars. But when he gets a job at a garage, he doesn't fumble around and mess things up as he did before. He knows how to do it right. That's how we should be when we learn from the Bible how to fix what's wrong in our lives.

- *Speak the Word.*

Two Scripture passages say this better than I ever could. "Pray also for me, that whenever I open my mouth, words may be given me so that I will fearlessly make known the mystery of the Gospel, for which I am an ambassador in chains. Pray that I may declare it fearlessly, as I should" (Ephesians 6:19-20, NIV).

"Peter and John answered and said to them, 'Whether it is right in the sight of God to give heed to you rather than to God, you be the judge, for we cannot stop speaking what we have seen and heard' " (Acts 4:19-20).

Peter and John were answering the authorities who had told them that they could no longer speak in Jesus' name. They had seen and heard the living Word of God, and it had become real to them. Don't just take in and experience Jesus. Give Him out.

God made you in His image. Be like a mirror, reflecting the goodness and truth He has given you so that others can see Him in you.

Once when my wife Tex and I returned from a week of meetings several hundred miles from our home, we found that our electricity had been out for the entire time. When I opened the freezer to see how my side of beef had fared, the stench told me the bad news. The hundreds of pounds of beautiful beef that I had counted on as a security blanket in time of need was now the worst mess I had ever smelled.

Cleaning up that freezer was unpleasant, and it hurt me to throw out all that expensive meat. Luckily, it wasn't a total loss. The Lord took pity on me while I was holding my nose with one hand and cleaning with the other. He gave me a bit of a parable. He led me to think of that meat as the Word of God. As beautiful and bountiful and expensive and helpful as that meat was, and as nutritious and life-giving as it could be, it was worthwhile only if it were used.

It had been stored for so long without the proper environment that its value had been lost, just as the value of the Word is lost when we don't keep it fresh by applying it in our daily lives. Then the Word becomes worthless.

So memorize, meditate, read, hear, study, pray, do, and speak the Word of God. Then you will be on your way to becoming like Jesus.

TELL

6
I Want to Tell the Whole World

A young woman who was just saved out of a life of drug addiction told me, "Sammy, becoming a Christian is so wonderful, I wish I could receive Christ over and over."

Of course, I told her that she couldn't, because when Jesus comes to live in your life, it's for eternity. "But I can tell you something that's just as great," I added.

"What's that?"

"Sharing Jesus with someone else and seeing that person receive Him."

She soon learned how to share her faith and began seeing God working in the lives of her friends and acquaintances. She could hardly express her joy. It was as if she were receiving Christ over and over, just as she had wanted. She had discovered a purpose for her life. Soul-winning is one of the most exciting things in the world, and the Bible says that he who wins souls is wise (Proverbs 11:30).

We often tell new Christians that they now have a

purpose in life, but have you ever stopped to think about just what that purpose is? We can talk about becoming like Christ—which is what this book is all about. But what is our purpose? If we're to be like Jesus, we should have a similar purpose to the one that brought Him to earth. Jesus described His purpose like this: "For the Son of Man has come to seek and to save that which was lost" (Luke 19:10).

Sometimes we think it would be better if Jesus snatched us up to heaven to be with Him the moment we receive Him as our Saviour. But He leaves us right where we are. Why? Just as Jesus' purpose was to seek and save the lost, it's ours too. Winning souls is one thing we can do on earth that we won't be able to do in heaven.

Jesus used many methods to share the Good News with people, and I'm convinced that any and all of these are good options for us. People argue too much over which methods are valid and which aren't; but if we study the ways Jesus did it, we can hardly go wrong.

The Friendship Approach

Back in Jesus' day, cultural taboos said a man didn't normally speak with a woman—but it was even more against the rules for a Jew to speak with a Samaritan. But that's just what Jesus does (John 4:5-29). Jesus, a Jew, began to build a relationship with the Samaritan woman by first breaking down the natural barriers. He spoke to her, casually asking for a drink of water.

Before long He was engaged in conversation and even spoke to her about her sin. Then He told her

I Want to Tell / 69

how to be a true worshiper of God. He started slowly, broke down the barriers, and then came on strong.

Are there people you know who need friends to care for them? Could you begin casually and slowly, and then share your faith with them? You wouldn't have to progress as quickly as Jesus Himself did—in fact, it might take months or maybe even years—but you could do it.

I know a girl who ran into one of her friends from high school. She hadn't seen her for years, but it quickly became obvious that they were quite different from each other.

Her friend had been into drugs and immorality, but this girl didn't start in preaching at her or even trying to tell her about her own faith in Christ. She simply talked with her as an old friend and asked if they could get together for lunch. During the first luncheon, her friend talked about herself and her disappointments in life. It was only natural that at the next lunch, she asked what my friend had been doing with herself. It was a natural opening to simply share what Christ had done for her and what He meant to her. No preaching, no talking down. Not even a mention of the other's problems and mistakes. The application was left unstated, yet it was apparent. When my friend asked her to come to church with her the next Sunday, her friend immediately accepted. I happened to be preaching that Sunday and went with the young people to a retreat later. Her friend was impressed by what she heard at church and received Christ at the retreat the following weekend. That's witnessing at its best.

Let me add a word of caution here, however: A Christian's first and most basic friendships should be with other Christians. The Bible says, "Do not be bound together with unbelievers" (2 Corinthians 6:14). There comes a time to reach out and build relationships with non-Christians for the purpose of leading them to Christ. But if too many of your friends are of the world, and too few are in Christ, you may find yourself being led into the ways of the devil.

The Indirect Approach

Jesus spent a lot of time at weddings and feasts and gatherings of tax collectors. He was with "sinners" so much that the Pharisees and scribes knocked Him for reaching out to those that "religious" people won't touch. But Jesus always said that He had come to heal not the healthy but the sick. He used such occasions to share the Good News. He didn't jump in and come on strong; He simply took advantage of situations.

When I was in college I worked part-time as interim pastor at a church in Pumpkin Center, La. If you think that sounds like it might be in the boondocks, you're right. Many of the kids in that area had nothing to do. So, I asked a few if they'd like to play some football Friday night. Sure enough, a bunch showed up.

We had played a while and had a good time. Afterward, I invited them into the church for a drink of water. I asked if they'd sit down a minute because I had something I wanted to tell them. I simply shared what Jesus had done in my life, and they listened. I did the same thing every Friday night for months.

I Want to Tell / 71

The crowds kept getting bigger and bigger and we even had car washes and other money-raising activities so we could buy athletic equipment. We played Ping-Pong and volleyball and softball and anything else anyone wanted. But when it came to a certain point in the evening, the kids wound up listening to the Gospel. I met the kids on their level and in three months, 40 had received Jesus.

Meeting People's Social and Physical Needs

The quickest way to get someone to listen to you is to meet his need. Witness to a hungry or hurt person without trying to help him, and he'll wonder just how your faith translates to everyday living. We give a lot of lip service to loving and caring, but we too often forget following up our talk.

When our ministry was headquartered in Chicago, we met people every day who were suffering for one reason or another. We could reach out to them and meet them, or we could pass them by like everyone else did. We chose to help. We had an extensive ministry to runaways, teens from all over the country whose train or bus or car ride landed them in Chicago. They were hungry, without money, homesick. They had nowhere to go and nothing to do.

We were able to work with the police department in helping these people find jobs, find their way home, get a place to stay, get some food or clothes. We tried to help them get their lives back together; and all the while, we shared Jesus with them. What would our witness have been worth if we had neglected their physical survival and psychological needs?

Of course, sometimes a direct witness is all you can give. It may plant a seed that the Holy Spirit will allow to grow later. Or to look at it another way, don't neglect to throw a drowning man a rope just because you don't have time to tie a life preserver to it.

We referred drug addicts to rehabilitation centers and halfway houses; and when we reached out, we always found the person's bigger need was for someone who cared, someone who loved him, someone who could help him straighten out his life. And we knew just the Person.

The Bold, Direct Approach.

In spite of my basic shyness, this approach is the one God has seemed to bless me with. I can preach with boldness, and often I can witness with boldness. The example of Jesus using this approach is best shown when Nicodemus, a ruler of the Jews, visits Jesus at night and compliments Him on His ministry.

Nicodemus tells Jesus he knows He must be from God, "for no man can do these signs that You do unless God is with Him" (John 3:2).

And how does Jesus answer? Does He say, "Hey, Nick, thanks. I appreciate that. I do the best I can with what I've got, and I appreciate your saying you noticed"?

Hardly. He immediately retorts that unless Nicodemus is born again, he will not enter the kingdom of heaven. That's strong; that's direct; that's straight shooting; there's no building a relationship here, no cutting corners. Because of the nature of our street ministry, we have found this approach very effective.

I like to use Gospel tracts, though I have met many Christians who don't. Sometimes we'll distribute a couple thousand leaflets, just to find the one person God has been dealing with who is ready for our witness. That may not sound practical, and there are many who say we turn off quite a few more than we reach for Christ. I agree that we have to use tact and sensitivity, but what if we chose not to pass out tracts because of whom we might offend? The Gospel *is* offensive to some people. The Cross offends. Jesus divides people. We feel that the one or two people in two hundred who will respond is worth all the effort. Notice Jesus didn't just come to save people. Before they could be saved, they had to be sought and found.

They are found by our seeking them out; and a

bold, direct approach will certainly tell you quickly who is ready and who isn't. If they are not hungry, don't feed them.

Sometimes a hard-hitting attack is best. Church visitation is another direct approach that many have found effective. A pastor friend from Oregon visits every home in his area and knocks on the door, sharing Christ with whoever answers and asks about their relationship with God.

One day he asked a man if he died right then, would he know for sure that he'd go to heaven.

"No," the man said. Then he added, "I am running for the state House of Representatives; and if you'll let me tell you why you should vote for me, I'll let you tell me all about it." My friend listened, and then shared, and that politician is now a born-again member of his church.

Another time the pastor met a man who said he was an atheist and slammed the door in the visitor's face. Some time later the pastor was out knocking on doors again. He began driving around, praying that God would reveal to him one person that He wanted to receive Him that day. "Surely there's one, Lord, in this city of a million people." The Lord led him to go back to the atheist's door.

He knocked. The man answered. "What are you doing here?" the man asked, not as belligerently as my friend might have expected.

"I was just driving around praying and asked God if there was one person in this town He wanted to save today. He led me to you." The man invited him in and told him an almost unbelievable story. It seems he and his wife had been arguing right then about the existence of God. While she was not a Christian, she believed there was a God. The man had just said, "The only way I would believe in God is if He would send that preacher back here to knock on my door right now."

That pastor believes that in every new subdivision he visits, there will be five or six families who are ready to receive Christ. The problem is finding out who they are. Sometimes, as in that story, the Lord leads him right to them. But usually, my friend makes it a point to hit every home. With that bold approach he finds out quickly who is ready to become a Christian and who isn't. By starting with the question about eternal life, he doesn't waste an uninterested party's time or his own.

None of the approaches Jesus used can be wrong, so we Christians need to quit arguing about which is best and which isn't. We can't convert someone to Christ without Him anyway. All we can do is let Him minister through us in whatever approach He chooses. Because of how He has worked in us, how we were raised, the type of spiritual training and teaching we received, or because of the particular gifts He's given us, we'll be more effective with one approach than another.

I encourage you to try approaches you aren't comfortable with. Don't use only your strengths, because then you might make the mistake of depending more on your own talent or ability than you do on God. Stretch yourself; force yourself to depend wholly on Him. Jesus always depended on the Father; so to be like Him we must do the same.

And don't be upset just because someone else uses another approach. The devil would love to make Christians angry with each other over such trivia. These methods are of Jesus; and we are to use them for His glory, not to argue about.

During His public ministry, Jesus at one point had many people suddenly quit following Him. It was because of something He said. It's found in John 6:44-45, 63, and it's the basis of His soul-winning: "No one can come to Me unless the Father who sent Me draws him, and I will raise him up on the last day. It is written in the prophets, 'And they shall all be taught of God.' Everyone who has heard and learned from the Father comes to Me. . . .

"It is the Spirit who gives life; the flesh profits nothing; the words that I have spoken to you are spirit and are life." After hearing this teaching, many of His disciples were not walking with Him anymore (6:66).

Jesus recognized that some were responding to Him in the wrong way. I find three different ways or levels people can respond to someone who witnesses to them.

The Three Levels of Responding to Witnessing

Many people have trouble understanding the God who is three Persons at once because they don't even understand the fact that every one of themselves is three persons. The Bible says that each person is a spirit, a soul, and a body. Paul wrote to the Christians, "Now may the God of peace Himself sanctify you entirely; and may your spirit and soul and body be preserved complete, without blame at the coming of our Lord Jesus Christ" (1 Thessalonians 5:23).

Let's define the three different levels this way: The body is physical, what you can see. The soul is the mind, the intellect, the emotions, the will. The spirit is the level at which a person can supernaturally respond to God. Jesus says a person can only come to Him if the Father draws him. We need to remember that we can be only instruments of the Holy Spirit's work.

Many witnessing experiences are presented and received physically, strange as that may seem. A person is excited by the person he's witnessing to and attracted to him or her. And the other person is responding on the same basis. That's why I generally recommend that guys witness to guys and girls to girls. I've seen many girls hurt when they found that guys they thought were interested in receiving

Christ were really just falling for them. Unless the Holy Spirit definitely leads you otherwise, I caution you against involving yourself in witnessing to a member of the opposite sex.

The second level is the level of the soul. Here we often find witnessing turning into intellectual debates, arguing, and emotional reactions. When you see someone come to Christ in tears and then he's thrown the whole thing over a few months later, you can assume that his was a reaction at one level alone, and it wasn't the spiritual level. That's not to say that a person shouldn't react emotionally when he's been born again. But it does mean that his whole life should change, not just his emotions.

Watch out when you find someone responding with intellectual arguments: It may be a smoke screen. He may say he is an agnostic or an atheist while he's simply rationalizing away a life he knows is against what God wants. Feeling guilty about it deep down, he pushes the guilt to the back of his mind by trying to convince himself that there may not be a God anyway.

When you have exhausted every intellectual, historical, and biblical argument and he still claims not to be convinced, perhaps the problem is not to be convinced, perhaps the problem is not in the intellect, but in the will. Or the spirit.

So what do we do when we're trying to witness to a person's spirit, but he's responding at the physical or soul levels? The Bible says, "For whatever God says to us is full of living power. It is sharper than the sharpest dagger, cutting swift and deep into our innermost thoughts and desires with all their parts, exposing us for what we really are" (Hebrews 4:12, LB).

God will take His Word and use it. Always ask for the Holy Spirit's aid in your witness. You may even want to say, "This is more than having an intellectual agreement or an emotional desire or even a physical attraction. This is where God touches you. You can't come to God unless He draws you. Do you sense God drawing you, or do you just want what I've got?"

Too many Christians try witnessing once and have a bad experience. Then they decide that God hasn't called them to witness. They should read the Great Commission again (Luke 9:60). We are all called to witness. We are to be like Jesus, and He shared the Good News. There is a time of learning and trial and error in every discipline.

When I learned to bowl, I read lots about it and even tried my approach at home before getting out to the lanes for real. I had it down real well, but guess what happened. The first several throws were gutter balls! My first game was a 30!

I finally realized that if I was going to be good at the game, I would have to practice for a while. A few years later I won the city championship and entered a national tournament. You may blow it the first few times you witness, but if you faithfully keep giving out the Good News, God will help you get better at it.

Some Practical Hints on Witnessing

If you feel butterflies before you share Christ, praise the Lord. Then you'll have to depend on Him wholly. If you're comfortable, you may be working on your own.

Be open to any opportunity to witness. For example, I was daydreaming while standing in line at a restaurant one evening. Apparently I was smiling, for a man I didn't know stopped as he walked by and said, "It can't be that good!"

"It really is," I replied, realizing an opportunity to tell this stranger about Christ.

"It can't be *that* good," he continued.

"Let me tell you a secret. It's better than that."

"If it's that good, what is it?" He was really interested now.

I then told him about Jesus Christ and what He'd done in my life.

Almost anything in life can be related to Jesus because the Bible says that He *is* the Life (John 14:6).

Develop a good, biblical presentation of how you received Christ; and hone it down to three minutes. Make sure it includes four things: (1) your life before Christ, (2) events that led to your conversion, (3) your actual conversion experience, and (4) the change in your life.

People don't want to discuss theology. They want to know what God has done for you. Your own testimony is a great place to start, if they are interested. Be sensitive. If a person does not want to hear it, don't push. You can often tell by a facial expression, a word, an action when it's time to stop. But don't stop too early either. I've seen people ready to receive Christ and the Christian decides to quit for fear that he'll appear pushy. The Holy Spirit will guide you if you stay open to His leading.

It's good to get people alone so they will not be embarrassed by talking to what their friends might call "those Christian weirdos." Jesus was a Gentleman and treated people with respect. If people do not want to hear you out, that's their choice.

Most of all, don't get upset, regardless of how people react. If they put you down, try to react in love. The more we share our faith in love, the more like Jesus we'll become.

CRUCIFIED

7
Me, Be Crucified?

Believe it or not, one of the ways we can become more like Jesus is by identifying with Him in His death, burial, resurrection, and ascension.

What? you're probably thinking. *I understand what it means to identify with Jesus' birth, to have a new life—to be born again. But how can I identify with His death, burial, resurrection, and ascension?*

I used to feel that way too. How could I possibly be like Jesus in these areas? Through the years I've spent a lot of time searching the Scriptures in my daily studies for answers to this question. Here's what God has taught me.

Paul wrote to his friends: "I have been crucified with Christ; and it is no longer I who live, but Christ lives in me; and the life which I now live in the flesh I live by faith in the Son of God, who loved me and delivered Himself up for me" (Galatians 2:20).

In Greek, the original language of this verse, the tense makes it refer to both past and present, so it should read, "I was and am still being crucified with

Christ," etc. Our old lives were crucified at salvation: "Therefore if any man is in Christ, he is a new creature; the old things passed away; behold, new things have come" (2 Corinthians 5:17).

Jesus told the religious leaders that if they did not repent, they would perish (Mark 1:15). When I received Jesus, I didn't know what "being crucified" meant; but I did know that I wanted Jesus more than all the booze and girls and parties and running around I had done. I wanted Him more than all my old ways.

Are you willing to let your old nature die? Many Christians are not. Think of it as if you were driving along and saw Jesus hitchhiking. You'd be appalled that the Son of God had to hitch a ride, so you'd pull over right away. But instead of Jesus getting in on the passenger's side, He comes around to your side and tells you to move over. Then He takes the wheel, but He doesn't stop there. Before going anywhere, He turns the car in the opposite direction.

Jesus won't come into a life that is not given completely to Him. Give up all rights to your old life, and He'll give you a new one. He'll turn you around. The old life will be dead. That's why I've been able to tell people all over the country that since I became a Christian, I've drunk all the booze I wanted to, swore all I wanted to, and run around with all the women I wanted to—but I've quit wanting to!

I don't want to be misleading. There are times when the old nature comes out in me and I am tempted, but God has changed my basic desires and direction. Now I don't want to continue in that old direction, even though Satan often tries to tempt me to it.

Me, Be Crucified? / 85

Two things will bring out the old nature quicker than anything else: praise and criticism. When someone compliments me and says, "Sammy, you're doing such a fine work, blah, blah, blah," my old nature often jumps out, and I start thinking, "Yeah, I guess I am pretty good." My egotistical nature has come out; and I must remind myself, "Sammy, you're dead." *The moment I think I'm somebody who has a lot to offer God, I quit acting like Jesus.* Jesus had no pride as He was obedient to death. When I am proud, I am not being like Him.

One day I called a pastor friend and he seemed cold, as if he didn't want anything to do with me. I called another friend and got the same reaction. Soon I discovered that a pastor in Germany had come to my hometown, before I returned from Germany, and had begun spreading lies about my ministry. I had black-and-white proof that he was lying, and my immediate response was to defend myself against this unjust criticism. My evil nature was really in control for a while as I prepared my defense. Then the Lord spoke to me.

"They lied about Me and criticized Me," He told me. "There was no fault in Me and I prayed, 'Father, forgive them; for they know not what they do.' If you want to know what it means to be crucified with Me, you must have that same attitude of love and forgiveness."

The Lord spoke so deeply to me that I asked His forgiveness for my defensive reaction.

Stephen took on the character of Jesus through his death. When he was stoned, he prayed a prayer much like Jesus had prayed on the cross: "Lord, do not hold this sin against them!" (Acts 7:60)

We should react even to untrue charges the way

Jesus did. A preacher friend that I respect says we should understand that the whole truth is much worse than any criticism we could receive, so we shouldn't get so upset about lies.

My old flesh is capable of anything. Jesus honors the truth because He is Truth (John 14:6). By the way, the truth came out in my ordeal; and my reputation was restored; but it wasn't because of anything I did. God continues to bless my ministry.

Buried with Christ

The Bible says, "Therefore we have been buried with Him through baptism into death, in order that as Christ was raised from the dead through the glory of the Father, so we too might walk in newness of life" (Romans 6:4).

And another verse says, "There is therefore now no condemnation to those who are in Christ Jesus" (8:1).

The psalmist says that God has separated our sin from us as far as the east is from the west (Psalm 103:12). Christians have been set free from the guilt of sin. When the old self was crucified, the sin was buried. Every sin, past, present, and future, was buried with Christ.

According to psychiatrists, one of every three hospital beds on this continent is occupied by someone with an emotional problem. And many of those problems can be traced to guilt. Why do so many people suffer such traumas from that feeling? Because they are guilty. They don't understand that Christ died to relieve them of all their sins. They try to push God and their sin and everything out of their minds, but it doesn't work. The guilt shows itself in all forms of illness.

There's only one way to deal with guilt, and that is to identify with Jesus who was the one Person who was completely innocent. He took on all our guilt so that we could be free.

Many people I know aren't effective Christians because they haven't realized that they could have their sins "buried" with Jesus.

This is often confusing because people don't understand the difference between God's *relationship* and His *fellowship*. We are God's children. He is our Father. That's our relationship with Him. The Bible says, "But as many as received Him, to them He gave the right to become children of God, even to those who believe in His name, who were born not of blood, nor of the will of the flesh, nor of the will of man, but of God" (John 1:12-13).

I have two children. They can get upset with me or I with them; they can run away, turn their backs on me, even disown me. But they are still my children. If they get angry with me and change their names, they are still my children.

Fellowship, as opposed to relationship, is the Christian's personal walk with God. Many things can affect that fellowship. If someone tells me that he's doubting his salvation, I'll ask first where he thinks sin is affecting his life. The devil attacks us at our weakest point.

But, no matter how badly we've blown our fellowship with God, we'll always be His children. He'll always be our heavenly Father. When we understand the difference between *fellowship* and *relationship*, we can learn how to be free from guilt and sin with Christ as our Protector.

Resurrected with Christ

Jesus' crucifixion and burial take care of our old nature and our sin, but His resurrection gives us victory. When God raised Jesus from the dead, sin, our old nature, Satan, hell, and death were defeated. Jesus was totally victorious.

When Jesus was crucified and buried, the disciples abandoned Him and denied Him. Peter lied; the intellectual Thomas needed proof. All turned away from Him except John. All were on the run in the wrong direction—till they saw the resurrected Christ. All but John died martyrs' deaths, according to tradition. What made the difference?

These early champions of the faith were referred to as men who upset the world (Acts 17:6). What changed them? They saw that Jesus had conquered man's worst enemy: death itself. They identified with the resurrected Christ, and they became victorious.

Raised Up with Christ

"If then you have been raised up with Christ, keep seeking the things above, where Christ is, seated at the right hand of God" (Colossians 3:1). We are qualified to sit at the right hand of the Father with Christ in the heavenly places! The Bible says, "Blessed be the God and Father of our Lord Jesus Christ, who has blessed us with every spiritual blessing in the heavenly places in Christ" (Ephesians 1:3).

Much of what it means to become like Jesus is simply to realize what He's already given us. The blessings He has for those who know Him are to be experienced daily through our lifetimes and eternity. That leaves room for a lot of growth, doesn't it? There is so much to enjoy and benefit from in Jesus!

"Set your mind on the things above, not on the things that are on the earth" (Colossians 3:2).

If we really seek the things in heaven, we can still live a practical life on earth. Prayer and communion with God in the Christian life involve seeking what is above and applying it to our everyday lives. The reason we mess up so often is that we try to handle things the way the world does instead of seeking God's will.

The more we discover about all the good things we have in Christ Jesus, the more we can enjoy becoming like Him, the true goal of discipleship.

WARFARE?

what is

8
Let's Hear Your Battle Cry

Too many people think that once a person has become a Christian, his life is cool, his problems go away, he never worries about anything.

But if being a Christian really means being like Christ, then a Christian crashes head-on into problems. There is real warfare in the Christian's life.

Ever since the Creation, Satan has been tempting man and has been successful in leading him to rebel against God. God will wipe out the rebellion eventually. But for the time being, "all have sinned and fall short of the glory of God" (Romans 3:23). Satan's effectiveness in destroying mankind is the reason Jesus came to die on the cross. The Bible says, "The one who practices sin is of the devil, for the devil has sinned from the beginning. The Son of God appeared for this purpose, that He might destroy the works of the devil" (1 John 3:8).

When Jesus Christ came to this planet, He didn't come to play games and have a good time; He came to do battle with the devil through His life, death, burial, and resurrection. If we are to be like Jesus, we must do the same.

The Bible records the first direct confrontation between Jesus and Satan (Matthew 4; Luke 4). Jesus combated the temptations of Satan by citing Scripture—and by being led by the Spirit. Having the Holy Spirit's guidance is necessary for battling the devil and resisting temptation.

Conflict can help us be more like Jesus. Paul writes, "Be strong in the Lord, and in the strength of His might. Put on the full armor of God, that you may be able to stand firm against the schemes of the devil. For our struggle is not against flesh and blood, but against the rulers, against the powers, against the world forces of this darkness, against the spiritual forces of wickedness in the heavenly places. Therefore, take up the full armor of God, that you may be able to resist in the evil day, and having done everything, to stand firm" (Ephesians 6:10-13).

Paul is saying that our war is with Satan, God's foe. We're in God's army, and we must be willing to go into battle. Some people are afraid to fight in this battle; but if they are to become like Jesus, they will have to.

Notice that Paul doesn't scream, "Charge!" He says to stand with Jesus. Paul continues: "Stand firm therefore, having girded your loins with truth, and having put on the breastplate of righteousness, and having shod your feet with the preparation of the Gospel of peace, in addition to all, taking up the shield of faith with which you will be able to extinguish all the flaming missiles of the evil one. And take the helmet of salvation, and the sword of the Spirit, which is the Word of God" (Ephesians 6:14-17).

"Gird Your Loins" with Truth

The girdle was one of the most important pieces of armor worn by soldiers in Paul's day, because all the other pieces were attached or related to it in some way. Since girdles were used to hold swords and other weapons, "gird your loins" really means, "get ready" with the Truth.

The Bible says that Jesus is Truth ("I am the Way, and the Truth, and the Life; no one comes to the Father but through Me" [John 14:6]). If you would put on Truth, you must put on Jesus. Become truthful and honest. John says that we should see sin the way God sees it: "If we say that we have no sin, we are deceiving ourselves; and the truth is not in us. If we confess our sins, He is faithful and righteous to forgive us our sins and to cleanse us from all unrighteousness" (1 John 1:8-9).

One of the hardest things to do in life is to admit when we are wrong. It's easy to see everybody else's faults, but seeing our own sin and dealing with it are necessary. When you notice a fault in someone else, ask God to point out the same fault in your life if it's there and you're not aware of it. It's amazing how many times I've had sin revealed to me this way.

A few years ago my wife and I had problems with stubbornness and our son. We tried everything. Then I asked God why my son Davey was so stubborn. The Spirit gently prodded, "Whom do you think he gets his stubbornness from?" God had to deal with my own bullheadedness and cleanse me of it before we could deal effectively with Davey.

The Breastplate of Righteousness

There are two types of righteousness: human and heavenly. Let's be sure when we put on the breastplate of righteousness that we're putting on the right type. Human righteousness—pride—is shoddy and will lead to destruction. Satan can attack and rip apart that type. The righteousness *God* gives people is seen in Jesus Christ.

Human righteousness isn't good enough to qualify anyone to meet God. But God had a solution: He became a man. He crashed through the wall between Himself and man.

Your Battle Cry / 95

Allow Him to be your righteousness. Otherwise, you'll be smashing into that wall.

The Preparation of the Gospel of Peace

Paul wrote about the Christian's footwear ("the Gospel of peace") while he sat in a Roman prison. He may have had a view of the shoes of the soldier who guarded him. What he would have seen were hobnail sandals that let the soldier change directions fast. When the enemy attacked, soldiers had to be agile. Paul seems to be drawing an analogy between these shoes and the Gospel, which can make us ready to fight Satan's attacks with the peace God gives those who love Him.

Again, what is our source of peace? The Bible says Jesus is the Lord of peace (2 Thessalonians 3:16). Paul writes to the Romans, "Therefore having been justified by faith, we have peace with God through our Lord Jesus Christ" (Romans 5:1). With such peace in our hearts, we'll be able to react quickly when God commands. If you don't have God's peace, you'll hesitate. When the enemy attacks, you won't be able to stand firm. Your victory will be lost.

There can be tremendous victory if our minds are filled with the peace of God. I remember one time in a city where I was holding a series of meetings. The local church body there joined with our staff people in some evangelistic street work. But there was one young man who would hold back and say he needed to pray about it first. A few hours later, when we returned from sharing the Lord, he was still there praying, trying to decide if it was what God would have him do.

A few days later we felt led to talk about Christ in the middle of a near riot. The young man said he didn't have peace about it again, and missed out on another spiritually uplifting time. It may have been God's will for the man to stay away from witnessing then. Maybe he really wasn't ready. I'm not trying to say that you should do the work of God without the peace of God in your heart. But if you don't get His peace settled in advance—before you have to make a decision to go out and work for Him or not—you'll hesitate and miss the experience of seeing God work. All for the lack of His peace.

There are things that will keep you from experiencing this peace, you know. If something is bugging you, read the Bible for the Holy Spirit's guidance. And bring your problem to God and let Him deal with it. He promises peace. That's what you need. The Bible says, "Be anxious for nothing, but in everything by prayer and supplication with thanksgiving let your requests be made known to God. And the peace of God, which surpasses all comprehension, shall guard your hearts and minds in Christ Jesus" (Philippians 4:6-7).

The Shield of Faith

We need faith, and faith comes from God. Jesus is "the Author and Perfecter of faith, who for the joy set before Him endured the cross, despising the shame, and has sat down at the right hand of the throne of God" (Hebrews 12:2).

The Bible says, "Therefore, since we have so great a cloud of witnesses surrounding us, let us also lay aside every encumbrance, and the sin which so easily entangles us, and let us run with endurance the race that is set before us" (Hebrews 12:1).

If you have ever run in or watched a track meet, you know that there are three important parts to any race: the start, the middle, and the finish. The race of life starts with Jesus. He is the Beginning, the Alpha. The difference between Christianity and man-made religions is that faith begins not with man's effort and religion, but only with God. "So faith comes from hearing, and hearing by the Word of Christ" (Romans 10:17).

Your own Bible study, quiet time with God, church, Sunday School, and other forms of fellowship and devotion will increase your faith as you hear the Word of God.

The best way for us to run the middle part of the race without losing is to keep our eyes on the finish. We have to keep our eyes on Jesus, trusting Him till we die. We're not to turn back, but to decide to follow Him all the way. Completely. Totally.

We often give my son a head start in races among our friends and family because he's the smallest and slowest runner. We give him enough of a head start that he can win if he runs as fast as he can. But every time he gets close to the finish line, he turns to see where everyone else is, and we pass him by.

If we get sidetracked by looking at each other and worrying about who failed us or hurt us, we will be defeated.

As for the finish, we can take an example from the first-century Christians who kept their eyes on Jesus to the end. Paul said, "I have fought the good fight, I have finished the race, I have kept the faith" (2 Timothy 4:7).

God wants those who don't quit in His army.

The Helmet of Salvation

We must be absolutely sure of our salvation, or when the enemy attacks we'll not be effective in prayer or witnessing. We'll be defeated if Satan can wedge in and cause doubt in this most important area of our lives. Faith is not made only of feelings which change every day. Faith is a continued assurance in our salvation through Christ.

Paul gave great advice to his young partner in witnessing: "For this reason I also suffer these things, but I am not ashamed; for I know whom I have believed, and I am convinced that He is able to guard what I have entrusted to Him till that day" (2 Timothy 1:12).

The Sword of the Spirit

The Word of God is our only offensive weapon. The Bible says of itself, that it is "living and active and sharper than any two-edged sword, and piercing as far as the division of soul and spirit, of both joints and marrow, and able to judge the thoughts and intentions of the heart" (Hebrews 4:12).

We need the sword of the Spirit because our battle is in the spirit, not in the flesh. The Bible puts it this way: "For though we walk in the flesh, we do not war according to the flesh, for the weapons of our warfare are not of the flesh, but divinely powerful for the destruction of fortresses" (2 Corinthians 10:3-4).

We tear down the devil's strongholds with the sword of the Spirit, just as Jesus tore down Satan with the Word (Luke 4). He combated temptation with the Word.

I've seen people try to use the Bible as a sword of man, using it to destroy people or to argue with them and put them down. That's not what God's Word is for. It's to help us submit to His will.

What a weapon! It's not designed for wasting in petty arguments among the brothers and sisters. Let's use this weapon for the purpose it was intended. Be eager to engage in combat with the enemy, for this will bring you to the place where you simply have to trust in Jesus. And by doing that, you will become more like Him.

SUBMIT

9
Submit!

When I led a bunch of guys on a cycling trip in Europe a few years ago, we tried a setup to make the going smoother. We broke into groups of four cyclists. Each group rode single file, with a leader in front. The leader broke the wind and watched the road for obstacles, while the other three riders bent low and covered the same distance with little wind resistance and less effort. The followers learned to trust the leaders for their very lives in this kind of cycling, for if the leader didn't avoid rough spots in the road, someone could fall and get seriously hurt.

When the leader got tired, he would swing wide and let the other three pass him and swing back into the last position. Then the person who was behind him became the leader.

Think of your life. If you decide you don't want to be a follower, you can pass up everyone and strike out on your own. But if the other people around work as a team, they will soon pass you because they conserve their strength and let their leader do the work. You learn to be a leader by being a follower till it's your turn.

Jesus learned to be a Follower before He became the Leader. Jesus' submission to His parents and His heavenly Father were important parts of His life.

We can look at Jesus' time on earth as a special series of stages. First He was born of God. Then He learned submission. He was given authority. He was obedient. Finally He did great things. By learning to submit to authority, Jesus learned the humility He needed to go through with the sacrifice of His life for ours.

That humility should be a part of our lives as well. Let's look at Jesus' life and see if we can be like Him as we go through those stages too. At first those stages might seem impossible, but I am convinced that everything Jesus did is to be an example to us. God wouldn't call us to be like Jesus unless becoming Christlike were possible through Him.

Born of God

When we are born again, we are born of God. But Jesus was born of God from the very beginning. An angel told Mary, in answer to her question of how she could possibly bear a child since she was a virgin—"The Holy Spirit will come upon you, and the power of the Most High will overshadow you; and for that reason the holy offspring shall be called the Son of God" (Luke 1:35).

Till we have been born again and God's Spirit has come to live in us, we'll never be able to understand the things of God or the real meaning of Jesus' life.

Submit! / 103

It was necessary for Jesus to be God's Son for His life and death to have meaning for us. Likewise, it's necessary for us to become sons of God through being born again for our lives to have meaning.

Submissive

At the age of only 12, Jesus was found preaching to the elders and the priests in the temple, amazing them with His wisdom (Luke 2:39-52).

When Jesus' parents found Him there, did He say to them, "Aw, stop treating Me like a kid. I can stay and teach all these guys a lot more."

No. He returned to Nazareth with His parents and "continued in subjection to them.... And Jesus kept increasing in wisdom and stature and in favor with God and men" (2:51-52).

Jesus was already wise in God's ways. He may have been able to begin His ministry even then. But the time wasn't right. He continued to live under His parents' authority, because that's the way God wanted it.

Gained Authority

About 20 years later—during Jesus' public ministry—"the multitudes were amazed at His teaching, for He was teaching them as One having authority and not as their scribes" (Matthew 7:28-29).

Where did this humble son of a carpenter get such "authority"? Jesus learned submission to authority in childhood. He earned the right to speak with authority as an adult. Those who will be in authority need first to learn what authority is and how to handle it—which they learn by observing how those in power use their clout.

Submission is an *attitude*—an attitude of respect for those God has placed over us. Can we expect to receive God's promises of peace and joy without meeting the conditions He puts on His gifts? I think not. One of the conditions is to honor our fathers and mothers.

Jesus did just that, and God gave Him authority. Jesus gained in wisdom and stature and in favor with God and man. This truth hints at the benefits offered to one who learns an attitude of respect and trust and honor for those in authority over him.

Does this mean that God will always protect the one in authority over us from telling us to do the wrong thing? Will He guarantee that this person will never fail us, never let us down, never sin? No. And if such a calamity should occur, are we then free to look for another authority? God might want us to sometimes, but not always.

God placed me under the authority of a pastor once, and when that pastor sinned, I wanted to bail out. I didn't want to be under his authority, but the Lord didn't let me run away. God assured me that I was there for a reason, and eventually I learned some deep truths about the Word of God. (The pastor eventually saw the wrong he was doing.) I learned from the man's mistakes. I learned that Satan can trap any man, no matter how godly, no matter how often he goes to church, no matter how spiritually mature he is.

You can gain authority by being in submission. You can state with authority the dangers of immorality, even though you're not personally guilty of every sin around. You can gain wisdom in dealing with certain problems even though you are not personally the victim. No matter who is in authority over you, whether it is an older Christian, a parent, a teacher, a pastor, a leader, or even a body of believers, you can grow in wisdom from his knowledge and sometimes even his mistakes.

If we submit to God, we can resist the devil and he will flee (James 4:7). When we are in submission to God and godly authority, we are protected.

Was Obedient

When Jesus first asked John the Baptist to baptize Him, John refused because he felt inadequate for such a job. But Jesus told him to "permit it at this time, for in this way it is fitting for us to fulfill all righteousness" (Matthew 3:15).

Jesus' baptism was an act of obedience.

Submission is an attitude, but obedience is an *act*. When we obey, we are *doing* what we know to be the will of God.

Jesus obeyed. And what happened? "After being baptized, Jesus went up immediately from the water; and behold, the heavens were opened, and He saw the Spirit of God descending as a Dove, and coming [to] Him, and behold, a Voice out of the heavens, saying, 'This is My beloved Son, in whom I am well pleased' " (3:16-17).

After the baptism, Jesus received the Holy Spirit (Luke 4:1). A person receives power from the Holy Spirit (Acts 1:8). Jesus received power to do and to be what God had intended. We need that same power.

But many people talk about the power of God today as if it is something that He zaps people with, pouring it out here and there all over the place. "Want some power? Here! Have some!"

God gives power to those who obey Him. You can tell God, "I'll go where You want me to go; I'll be what You want me to be; I'll do what You want me to do." But it's only when He sees that you're serious about serving Him completely that He will allow you to experience His power.

Many new Christians become discouraged when no one receives Christ as a result of their witness. In the first three months of our ministry in Chicago, no one received Christ, and hardly anyone was even interested in hearing what we had to say.

Before, down South, we had seen hundreds decide to live for Jesus. Now, in Chicago, nothing. I was ready to quit. I prayed, "God, did I do something wrong? Didn't You lead me here?"

God assured me I was in His will. I believe He wanted to see if I would continue to obey Him in spite of fruitless efforts. God is looking for obedience. I obeyed and continued to minister.

Obedience releases the power of God on our lives. But what happens when obedience to God and submission to authority conflict? If someone in authority over you tells you to do something contrary to the Word of God, you've got a real problem. Don't be so naive that you think God would never let this happen. So then what? Do you submit to the authority and be disobedient to God?

We need to understand obedience so we can handle this dilemma the right way. The best example of the balance between submission and obedience is in Peter's life. He walked with Jesus and learned both submission and obedience. When the high priest questioned Peter and the apostles, Peter told him, "We must obey God rather than men" (Acts 5:29).

Was Peter then being unsubmissive? No. Remember that obedience is an action and submission is an attitude. Peter and John told their accusers to judge whether or not they were doing wrong according to the law and that if they had to suffer for it, they would. "For we cannot stop speaking what we have seen and heard" (Acts 4:20).

To disobey God in order to be submissive to man is not what God intends. Some people obey God while bitterly rebelling against authority. This is not pleasing to God either. Maintain your honor and respect of those in authority, but obey God at all costs.

Great Works

After Jesus was born of God, developed an attitude of submission, and acted out His obedience, He then did great things. "Believe Me that I am in the Father, and the Father in Me; otherwise believe on account of the works themselves" (John 14:11). Jesus' great works took place after He had been through the other stages.

One caution: Just because you're submissive doesn't mean you're likely to perform a miracle a day or preach great sermons. It might not be God's will for us to have our names in lights. But our real reward shouldn't be in earthly works but in eternal life.

The Series of Stages is Repeated

Jesus' life actually went through two series of stages. First He was submissive to His parents. Then He submitted to His Father's will. Submitting to God's will led Him to the ultimate act of obedience, dying on the cross—more than just a matter of returning home from Jerusalem and the temple with His parents.

God asked for His life. That went against His humanness. It would hurt. After questioning and praying to God to let Him off without having to die, Jesus was obedient. His submission led to obedience.

In the same way, if we are obedient to our Father, He will grant us the power and strength we need in our lives. A lot of us are cool as long as everything is smooth. Can we obey as Daniel obeyed, even at the threat of being sent into a den of lions? (Daniel 6:6-22) Or as the Old Testament people Shadrach, Meshach, and Abed-nigo who were sentenced to burn in a furnace? (3:16-23) Jesus and these men were obedient when things got rough. We should be willing to follow Jesus' example even when we don't feel well, even when things aren't going our way, even when what we stand for might endanger our lives. Few of us will ever be called to such extremes, but the examples of these Bible men should make us think twice when we "just don't feel like it."

We can get power and authority if we are obedient to God's will. What a thrill to have even the chance to be like Jesus. Let's use that power—His power.

GROWTH

10
The Process of Growth

My daughter Renee was born in a small hospital in the Swiss Alps. I was privileged to witness the entire labor and delivery process. Being there was a tremendous, beautiful experience. When I saw that little life come into being, I was overcome with a sense of awe at my responsibility to help her grow physically, mentally, emotionally, and spiritually.

She was born at one specific second of a particular minute on a certain day of a month in a year my wife and I will never forget. In the same way, when we are born spiritually, Christ comes into our lives, makes us new, and begins His work in us. It happens at a specific time. You may not know or remember the exact day and hour, but there was a point in your life when the bond with God was tied.

Then, just as Renee began to grow, new Christians should grow. Had my wife and I wished Renee luck and left her atop one of the Alps, we'd have been guilty of murder, even though we did our part by bringing her into the world. She was a newborn baby, helpless, totally dependent on us.

When Jesus was talking with Nicodemus, He compared being born physically with being born spiritually. Jesus said, "That which is born of the flesh is flesh; and that which is born of the Spirit is spirit" (John 3:6).

This comparison was a giant step in helping Nicodemus understand Jesus' mission on earth. We can use the same analogy in understanding what God wants to do in our lives.

Many of you have decided that while being like Jesus looks pretty good, it's too heavy for you. You can't handle it. Maybe you've tried studying your Bible and praying every day, yet you don't seem to be growing spiritually. You wish God would make you a more mature Christian, a supersaint, a spiritual giant overnight. But it doesn't work that way. Baby boys aren't born as six-foot-two, 275-pound tackles ready physically and mentally to start for the Dallas Cowboys. (Mothers all over the world are thankful for that!)

Great men and women of God are not made in one minute, week, or even a few years. Yes, they become children of God in an instant, but their spiritual maturity comes about through a lifetime of God working in their lives. We're born physically as babies. And we are born spiritually the same way. So the first stage of Christian life is the "baby" stage.

Getting Rid of Baby Fat

If you became a child of God many years ago but have not grown spiritually mature in any way, you

The Process of Growth / 113

are still a baby Christian and have lots of baby fat. Of course, you should be concerned about your lack of growth, but don't feel alone or unique. Regardless of a person's age or how long he has been a Christian, he can still be a baby. And, sad to say, our churches are full of spiritually flabby babies.

In most cases, the lack of physical growth is irreversible. Not so with spiritual midgets. If you have a normal brain and mind, there is no reason why you can't begin to grow spiritually as soon as you commit yourself to it.

There are places in Scripture where Christians are scolded for being babes in Christ. But these are cases where they were still in spiritual diapers when they should have been mature Christians. There is nothing wrong with being a baby Christian if you are a new Christian. It's a natural stage in your development. But Paul chastises the Christians at Corinth for their baby fat. He says, "I . . . could not speak to you as to spiritual men, but as to men of flesh, as to babes in Christ. I gave you milk to drink, not solid food; for you were not yet able to receive it. Indeed, even now you are not yet able, for you are still fleshly, and are you not walking like mere men?" (1 Corinthians 3:1-3)

Don't think that the term "babes in Christ" is in itself a put-down. For these Christians who should have been maturing, it was. But for a new Christian, it is simply a descriptive term.

Think of the characteristics of the physical baby. A baby cannot feed himself. The same is true spiritually. One of the most important things a baby Christian can do is to hook himself up with a local body of believers where the Word of God is preached as truth, where Jesus Christ is honored,

114 / Reproduced by Permission

and where the people love one another.

Jesus said, "Man shall not live on bread alone, but on every word that proceeds out of the mouth of God" (Matthew 4:4). The Word of God is the Christian's food. At first you may not be able to feed yourself, any more than a newborn infant can feed himself. That's why God gave the Church people such as apostles and prophets and teachers and pastors and evangelists to teach us the Word of God (Ephesians 3:5).

You'll never become a strong Christian till you find people who love Jesus and can feed you.

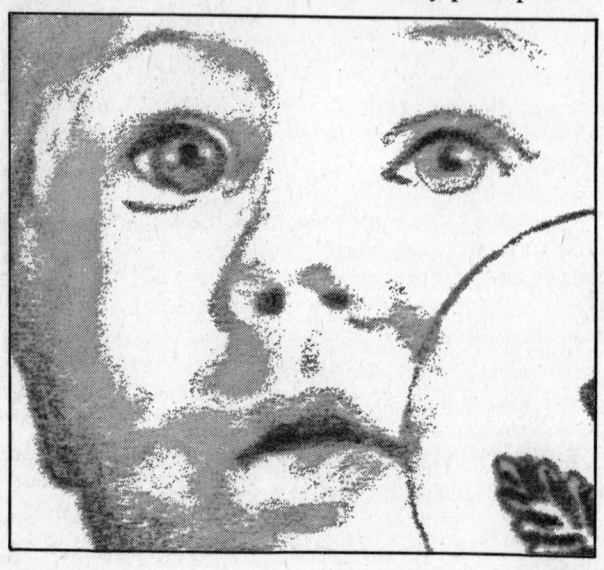

What is a baby fed? Milk. The writer of the Book of Hebrews says, "For though by this time you ought to be teachers, you have need again for someone to teach you the elementary principles of the oracles of God, and you have come to need milk and not solid food. For everyone who partakes only of milk is not accustomed to the Word of righteousness, for he is a babe. But solid food is for the mature, who because of practice have their senses trained to discern good and evil" (Hebrews 5:12-14).

It's important for a baby to start on milk. And a baby Christian is in trouble if he looks for milk in the first or last book of the Bible—as we have talked about earlier. I recommend starting in the middle of the Old Testament with the Psalms, or with the Gospel of John in the New.

Don't try to understand all the deep things of God right from the beginning. Babies don't start with T-bone steak. They stick with milk and strained foods till they get teeth and are beginning to learn to walk.

A baby cries and throws temper tantrums when he doesn't get his way. Isn't this also true of immature Christians? Older Christians should allow for a bit of childish behavior on the part of new Christians.

Remember, there's nothing wrong with baby Christians acting like baby Christians. The problem comes when the supposedly mature, strong ones begin acting like babes. God doesn't get upset with baby Christians unless they still have baby fat when they should be strong enough to teach other babies to be mature. It is wrong to continue as a baby and not to move to the next level of maturity.

John puts Christians into three categories: fathers, young men, and children. "I am writing to you, fathers, because you know Him who has been from the beginning. I am writing to you, young men, because you have overcome the evil one. I have written to you, children, because you know the Father" (1 John 2:13-14).

John could have been writing to men at different ages and stages in physical development; but based on the context, I believe he was writing to Christians of different stages of spiritual development. With that in mind, the next stage of growth in our development as true disciples, or ones like Christ, is the "child" stage.

The Wobbly Stage

Childhood is a time of learning. It is a time of development from the baby stage. And just as a physical baby must learn four basic things in order to survive, so must the baby Christian in order to mature.

- *Solid Food*

First, the physical baby learns to eat solid food. Many Christians get hung up when they try anything more than the Milk of the Word. They don't understand why they can't grasp the Word's meaning for their lives right away. They don't understand why they aren't more disciplined and productive in their study and meditation and memorization. They probably don't remember the problems they had with their first two or three dozen attempts to eat solid foods as children.

The first thing a small child may do when a plate is set before him is fling it at Daddy. Then something gets flung Mommy's way. Then brother or sister is the victim as the child tries to find his mouth with oversize spoonfuls of mashed-up food. Eating is awkward and frustrating because it requires coordination and muscles that have not yet been developed. And there's only one way to develop them—through practice. The new Christian who gives up daily Bible study and prayer because he seems to be growing too slowly is quitting too soon. When Christian growth seems the most frustrating, that's the time to dig in and stick it out till Bible study and prayer become natural.

That's something for us to remember when we are discipling a new Christian. When he gets discouraged, we should give him advice and encouragement to keep going.

The more a baby learns, the more he eats; and the more he eats, the more he grows. Then he is ready to learn to walk.

- *Walking*

Paul says, "Walk by the Spirit, and you will not carry out the desire of the flesh" (Galatians 5:16).

How does a child learn to walk? He takes a step or two and falls on his face. Then he gets back up, takes another step or so, and falls on his head. He falls so many times that parents often wonder if he'll ever get it right. But it isn't the falling that is teaching him to walk. It's the getting up and trying it again.

After awhile, the tears are gone, the bruises have healed, and the child is walking several steps at a time. Suddenly he's running. Then he's climbing on chairs and stairs and tables and who knows what else.

The spiritual process is similar. There are falls and failures and bruises and crying. Too many new Christians—and even some older ones—believe that the Christian life is going to be problem free. They think they'll never blow it, never fail God.

Wrong. Being a Christian doesn't mean that you will never sin again or fail God. You will fall, but now you can pick yourself up and get back in the race. Oh, you may cry over your failure as you did when you were a wiggly and wobbly child. And you may think you're falling an awful lot for someone who's supposed to be a "flawless" Christian. But the more you get back up and practice walking in the Spirit, the more effective you'll be.

The worst thing for a new believer is not the falling. It's failing to get back up and claiming you haven't fallen in the first place. "If we say we have no sin, we are deceiving ourselves, and the truth is not in us" (1 John 1:8). The Bible says, "All have sinned and fall short of the glory of God" (Romans 3:23). The key is getting up after failing and falling. And how do you get up?

The answer: "If we confess our sins, He is faithful and righteous to forgive us our sins and to cleanse us from all unrighteousness" (1 John 1:9).

The moment you fail God, admit it. Make no mistake about it, admitting that you are wrong is hard to do. But we must agree with God that we have sinned, and we must be willing to turn from the sin. Then He promises to take the sin away from us by His supernatural power.

Often when children get caught doing something wrong and are about to get spanked, they plead so convincingly, "Oh, Daddy, please don't spank me! I'm sorry; I won't ever do it again!" But is that repentance or simply dread of the punishment? Be sure you are willing to turn from your sin and are not simply pleading a pardon from the punishment.

Don't just be sorry you were caught. Be willing to turn from sinning against God Himself. God will forgive you; He will lift you back up again to walk with the Spirit.

- *Talking*

A baby learns to talk. The spiritual counterpart of talking is learning to share one's faith. "But you shall receive power when the Holy Spirit has come on you; and you shall be My witnesses both in Jerusalem, and in all Judea and Samaria, and even to the remotest part of the earth" (Acts 1:8).

A "witness" is someone who tells what he has seen, heard, or experienced. Failure to develop in this area can stunt a Christian's spiritual growth. The way to learn to share your faith is to spend time with somebody who is doing it. Young children who have older brothers or sisters learn to talk sooner than children raised without them. In my own Christian life, I learned to witness by spending time with a man who shared his faith in Christ with almost everyone as naturally as he breathed.

At first, telling someone about Christ will be awkward and difficult, like a baby's first faltering one-syllable attempts. But it isn't long before a baby is jabbering away!

Learn to express what God has done for you. I don't completely buy this idea of witnessing by the type of lives we live. Certainly, we don't want to sin against God or embarrass Him. But how many people do you know who are Christians today because somebody simply "lived the Christian life" before them? Let's not hoodwink ourselves into thinking that our job is only to live the Christian life and it's someone else's job to spread the Good

News of Jesus Christ. That's a cop-out. Before a person can become a Christian, he must be born again. This means he must hear and know and understand what it means to receive Christ.

- *Sharing*

The fourth crucial learning experience for children and wobbly Christians is learning to share. "For God so loved the world that He gave His only begotten Son, that whoever believes in Him should not perish, but have eternal life" (John 3:16).

That's probably the most beautiful and well-known verse in all of Scripture—it tells about the character of God. He is the good God. He is the giving God. He is the God of love. He shares the best of what He has with us. And to be like Jesus, who is also God, we must learn to share our talents and abilities with other Christians for God's kingdom. This is a difficult stage, just as it is in the life of a physical child.

Have you ever noticed that children can be playing together, and having no problems till a new child comes along and picks up a toy the others have been ignoring all along? Suddenly that ignored toy becomes valuable property, with each claiming ownership and demanding to play with it right then. It happens every time. Somehow, if a certain toy is important to the new child, it is important to the others. One of the hardest things to teach a child is to share something. Each of us is born self-centered, and this trait surfaces early.

It's just as hard to convince wobbly Christians that they are to share their talents and abilities with other Christians. The body of Christ can only be mirrored in a body of people, for some people will have some of His attributes and others will have others. If you are part of a local church body and haven't contributed the gift God has given you, whether it is speaking, organizing, showing mercy, helping out, whatever, you're stifling the nature of Christ in the body.

Artistic gifts can be used in unique and creative ways. Almost anything God has blessed us with can be shared to strengthen and unify the body. Perhaps yours is the gift of giving. The more you earn, the more you will be able to give. It's important to spiritual growth that a Christian learns to give back to God a portion of what he has received from Him.

The Overcomer Stage

According to Scripture, a young man should be an overcomer, a victor (1 John 2:13-14). That's why it is important to learn three major points about this stage. A young man has learned to eat, walk, talk, and share; but he goes further. He finds personal victory in his Christian life. I believe God wants every born-again believer to find that victory. "For whatever is born of God overcomes the world; and this is the victory that has overcome the world—our faith" (1 John 5:4).

Faith is the victory that overcomes the world. Young men—and young women—succeed through trusting in Jesus, not by depending on their own strength or abilities. The young person who "overcomes" has learned to place his entire trust and confidence in Jesus for his very life. He has the attitude of Paul when he writes, "For to me, to live is Christ, and to die is gain" (Philippians 1:21).

Second, such a young person has overcome the world and Satan by trusting in Jesus.

Third, the young person becomes strong by walking with God. Just as a young person develops physical muscles, so a spiritual person develops inwardly. He is strengthened by walking in the Spirit, building on the foundation laid at the child stage when he first learned to walk.

Each small victory can bring on an even greater victory. You'll become great and strong in the major areas of the faith life after you have experienced victories in smaller areas. The young person has done this, but he is not yet at the parent stage.

The Father Stage

A physical father or mother is one who is strong and has the capacity to reproduce. Spiritual parents have given themselves to God and can produce spiritual children who will one day become fathers and mothers themselves.

As I have said earlier, you don't just leave a baby to fend for itself. You teach it and help it grow. Spiritually, we should take responsibility for our "children" and make sure they are instructed so they can grow in the grace and knowledge of Jesus. Their goals are to stand on their own, walk in the Spirit, be victorious, and learn to reproduce themselves spiritually.

Our ultimate goal is to help them become like Jesus—the same goal we should have for ourselves.

MULTIPLY

11
Spiritual Multiplying

After Jesus told His disciples to "go into all the world and preach the Gospel to all creation" (Mark 16:15), they responded by dedicating their lives to that goal.

They didn't win the whole world over at once. But they did add 3,000 or 5,000 at a time to the Church, as recorded in the Book of Acts. The Word of God kept on spreading, and the number of disciples continued to increase greatly in Jerusalem (Acts 6:7).

God used the disciples as instruments for His glory. Like them, we are to grow in Christ not simply for our own personal victory, though that's important. We also should introduce others to Jesus and train them so they can do the same.

Too many Christians have become blessing sponges. They go to church, attend Bible studies, and memorize Scripture. They soak up all kinds of spiritual things without ever letting anyone else share what's been happening in their lives.

God created us for a specific purpose: to help others know the Good News of Jesus Christ and to live like Him.

The first thing God told Adam to do after creation was to "multiply and subdue the earth" (Genesis 1:28). This was before Adam sinned and when he had a perfect personal relationship with God. God wanted a world full of people who would live for His honor and glory.

But then God destroyed almost all of the very people He created (Genesis 7). Why? Because the people weren't honoring Him. He wanted people who wanted to be like Him. That's the basis for spiritual multiplication.

Adam and Eve started two lines of people. One was displeasing to God (the descendants of Cain), and from the other came the salvation of humanity (Seth's descendants). Cain killed Abel and broke God's teaching and commandments.

The other line—from their son Seth—prayed to the Lord and fellowshiped with Him. From this line came holy men such as Enoch and Noah. Adam and Eve finally did what God told them to do: to give Him more godly people.

Two Ways to Multiply

The first and most obvious way to multiply spiritually is through your family. Scripture is full of instructions for raising godly families. God's first command to Noah and his family was the same one He had given to Adam: "And God blessed Noah and his sons and said to them, 'Be fruitful and multiply, and fill the earth'" (Genesis 9:1). (Notice that this commandment was made to Adam and Eve before they sinned, and to Noah and his family after they had proven faithful.)

One group of churches praised itself at its 50th anniversary convention for having doubled in size since its beginning, from 50,000 to 100,000. However, someone quickly figured that if every parent in the denomination had led his children to Jesus and they did the same with their own children, the Christians in those churches would have numbered close to 400,000! What they thought had been a wonderful gain had been a horrible loss.

We are often satisfied with a few additions to our churches when we should be multiplying through our families. God has laid a heavy responsibility on fathers and mothers to train their children for His glory. My wife and I are convinced that we are not to simply preach and minister unless we are doing just that in our home.

God has blessed churches where members have caught this vision of discipling through the family. There is a revival that has flourished for several years among young people in East Germany. One of the ways God has worked there is through prayer and multiplication. A group of 60 kids grew to 100, then to 500, then 1,000, then 1,500; and recently more than 10,000 met at one time.

A second type of multiplication is through the Church. The Apostle Paul knew about this second type of multiplying. The one-on-one family-type of multiplication is found in the New Testament, right along with that of church body to church body. Paul spells out the whole point of his efforts to disciple Timothy: "And these things which you have heard from me in the presence of many witnesses, these entrust to faithful men, who will be able to teach others also" (2 Timothy 2:2).

I'm afraid we have too many day-care centers for baby Christians. We get 'em saved, then throw 'em in with a group and say, "Mature!" We need follow-up. I know of one church that assigns a mature Christian to every new Christian. The older Christian meets with him, talks with him, teaches him, and nurtures him.

Before you can reproduce yourself in others, through the family or through the Church, you have to be spiritually mature. You must go through several steps before you have reached that level of maturity, which I talked about in the last chapter.

Be Picky!

When you've shed your Christian baby fat and you're ready to start discipling others, be sure you choose your potential disciples carefully. Satan would love for you to waste your time on people who have little interest in becoming Christians. You'll wind up frustrated and discouraged. If God has poured enough of Himself into you that you are ready to do the same with someone else, be careful to choose people who are:

- *Faithful.*
If a person isn't serious, you can't teach him. He must want to know Christ better.

- *Teachable.*
The hardest person to disciple is the one who thinks he has all the answers and knows everything al-

Spiritual Multiplying / 129

ready. He doesn't need you. A teachable person will have a basic commitment to Christ—and to your teaching.

● *Able to teach others.*
Get your disciple to take notes because as he learns he'll have an outline to follow when he teaches others. Keeping a notebook isn't for his own benefit. Remember that the goal is for him to disciple others as well as to mature personally.

As you disciple one-on-one, make sure you don't leave out the Church. We can see the fullness of Jesus' character only when an entire body of believers is using its gifts for God. One person may be a prophet and may preach, while someone else who is a teacher will explain the preaching. And the one with the gift of mercy will help those who need help.

Multiplication must come through the Church, the body, even if it begins one-on-one. Too often we see people who are heavily into evangelism go to strictly evangelistic churches. And people who are into teaching go to heavily instructional churches. Other people who are strong in praise go to churches where praise is central. I believe God is looking for a fellowship of people who realize that all of this should be balanced in a local body. We complement and balance one another.

A Word of Warning

When you really get an idea of what God wants to accomplish through spiritual, scriptural multiplication, you will be in danger of persecution. The Children of Israel were following the command God had given to Adam and Eve and to Noah and his family: "But the sons of Israel were fruitful and increased greatly, and multiplied, and became exceedingly mighty, so that the land was filled with them" (Exodus 1:7).

But then trouble comes. "Now a new king arose over Egypt, who did not know Joseph" (1:8). The Children of Israel were persecuted and afflicted by taskmasters. Their sons were threatened with death because the Israelites were bigger and mightier in number than the Egyptians, and they were feared.

When we multiply, Satan will send persecution, but we should react the way the Israelites did: "But the more they afflicted them, the more they multiplied and the more they spread." (Exodus 1:12).

Rest assured that becoming like Christ, giving up all to become one of His and to multiply as He has commanded, will mean you'll have to give up things and endure things. The cost will be great.

COST

12
The Cost of Being like Christ

"Jesus Freak," "Goody Good," "Straight," "Not with It," "Uncool," "Square," whatever.

These are a few of the words that have caused young Christians over the years to wonder if trying to be Christlike is really worth it.

As we become more and more serious about becoming like Christ, we notice how different we seem to be from the rest of the world.

Know something? We *are* different.

And it hurts sometimes.

But Jesus teaches that in order for us to follow Him, we should "deny ourselves." We should forget some of the things the world around us tells us are important. In other words, before we decide that becoming like Christ is the thing for us to do, we should consider how much all this is going to cost.

"For which one of you, when he wants to build a tower, does not first sit down and calculate the cost, to see if he has enough to complete it? Otherwise, when he has laid a foundation, and is not able to finish, all who observe it begin to ridicule him, saying, 'This man began to build and was not able to finish' " (Luke 14:28-31).

As we build our lives on the foundation of Jesus Christ Himself, will we honor Him or embarrass Him because we never counted the cost and bailed out when the going got rough? Many people say, "Oh, yes, I'm going to be His disciple." But where are they now? They didn't understand what being like Christ would cost them.

When some of us realize how expensive it is, we'll quit.

It's important to know and understand that what God begins, He finishes. One of my favorite verses, and one I quoted earlier, is, "For I am confident of this very thing, that He who began a good work in you will perfect it till the day of Christ Jesus" (Philippians 1:6).

So, what is the cost of becoming more like Christ? If we sit down to calculate the cost before we decide to follow Him all the way, as the Master suggests, what things will wind up on our list? We should realize at the outset what being a true Christian takes. Then when the hurt comes, we won't be surprised.

Time

True discipleship takes time. Jesus spent time with the Twelve Disciples (Mark 3:14). You should realize at the outset the time being a Christian takes. Time is the one thing we can never have back, once it has been invested or wasted. I've thought back often to my high school days and wished that I had been a Christian then. One of my greatest aims is to help young people get to know Jesus, and I was with 2,000 young people every day for four years. Those days are gone, spent on booze and fun and activities and grades and sports. We must be careful that we don't miss becoming like Jesus just because we won't take the time.

It takes time to pray 30 minutes or so in the morning. But time must be given for doing that. The same is true for Bible study and memorization or meditation. Studying is not something we can do when we get a minute or two here or there. We must plan for our study and give it the time it requires, more than just three or four or five minutes a day.

Fellowship takes time too. Growing, studying, loving, being with God's people—being to them what God wants you to be—all take time. And as you commit yourself to sharing your faith in Christ, that takes time too.

Something has to give. Something may have to go. We can't do all that we used to and still do enough to become a true disciple of Christ. There simply aren't enough hours in a day. Many times you will be choosing what God wants over something evil. That's rather easy. But there will be times when you will find yourself choosing better over good and best over better. And this will be difficult. Many things you will have to give up will be things that are not wrong in themselves. They just crowd out the things of God.

Pain

If you want to be like Jesus, you'll hurt. It's as simple as that. There are two types of pain you will suffer. One is from the world, the non-Christians. A pagan cannot understand the things of the Spirit of God, so he will not understand when you begin to grow in Christ.

An unbeliever may take some jabs, have some fun, and might even try to hurt you, perhaps even physically (though this is rare in America). When the pain comes, remember the godly attitudes of both the Saviour Himself and Stephen. Jesus begged the Father to forgive the people who were crucifying Him because they didn't know what they were doing (Luke 23:34). And Stephen prayed for God to forgive those who were stoning him (Acts 7:60).

When Moses delivered God's message, "Let my

people go," Pharaoh had a good laugh. Moses had a message and a mission and was to be the deliverer of a life-changing message. But he was not only ignored and laughed at—he was rudely thrown out. Pharaoh told him, in effect, "Not only am I not going to let them go, I'm going to make it worse for them" (Exodus 5:2-9).

You'll find people who will do similar things to you. You may be laughed at and ridiculed and put down for your faith, but this is not necessarily a bad thing.

Peter cautions us not to get punished or persecuted for something wrong or obnoxious. Make sure what you're doing is for the sake of Jesus and righteousness. When you live a godly life, you may be persecuted. Don't react or get your feelings hurt or be ugly. React in the Spirit and in love of Jesus Christ.

The second type of pain you will suffer will come from other Christians, and this is the hardest to take because it is the hardest to understand. Being hurt by other Christians was one of the biggest stumbling blocks to me early in my Christian life. I could not understand the pain that came from within the body of believers. I had been under the impression that Christians would never turn their backs on you. Again, however, we can look to Moses' life to see that you can't depend on anyone completely, except Jesus.

When Moses returned to demand the release of the Children of Israel, he was opposed not only by the ruler this time, but also by the elders of the captives he wanted to free. The captive elders hadn't been where he had been. They had not been in the desert wilderness; they had not seen the glory of God and heard His voice. Pharaoh made it tougher after Moses' last visit, so this time the elders told Moses to cool it.

"You're comin' on too strong," they told him in effect. "You're not helping. Leave us alone. Our situation is horrible, but we were better off before you started making trouble."

Moses cried to the Lord. The elders' comments hurt him deeply, just as they would you or me. But at the same time, Moses did not give up on freeing the Children of Israel. When other Christians hurt us, we are not to run away from them. We should expect problems and pain as part of the cost of true discipleship.

I imagine it hurt Jesus when His own disciples didn't understand Him. It hurt when Peter tried to talk Him out of the suffering He was to face in Jerusalem. It must have hurt Jesus to know that He would be betrayed and then denied. But He didn't give up on His people.

The pain gets more intense and complicated and deeper the more you become like Jesus. You may even wonder, as Jesus did, if God hasn't forsaken you. Are you beginning to see that being like Christ is no game? To be like Jesus means to struggle through some deep, deep water.

"It's Worth It"

Following Jesus will mean losing your life to Him. Jesus told His disciples, "If anyone wishes to come after Me, let him deny himself, and take up his cross, and follow Me. For whoever wishes to save his life shall lose it; but whosoever loses his life for

My sake shall find it" (Matthew 16:24-25). We must be willing to abandon ourselves totally to God.

So many Christians have not come to that point. For several years I have worked in Communist countries where 90–95 percent of the converts follow through and mature as Christians. Their secret? Most of them count the cost of discipleship *before* they sign on. And once they have counted the cost and know the possibilities, they know exactly what they are getting into. They are not surprised by the persecution. They know their lives and futures and families are in danger. They know they will be watched and hassled and threatened. They decide at the outset that they will lose their lives for God's sake, by either dying or giving up some of their freedoms.

I spoke to a large group of underground Christians in the East German city of Dresden a few years ago. Afterward a girl asked me to pray with her. As we prayed, there was a very unusual movement of the Spirit of God in that place, and I noticed that all of the young people were on their knees praying.

When I finished prayer with the girl, I went around and prayed with each of the other young people. They had different needs and concerns, but there was a common thread at the end of every one of their prayers. I don't mind telling you, their prayers moved me and I will never forget them. One prayed for salvation, one prayed for recommitment, one prayed for Christ to take full control of his life. But at the end of each prayer was a German phrase, *"egal was es costet,"* meaning, "whatever it costs."

Six Czech young people, whom I had heard pray just that very phrase, stood in a Communist party

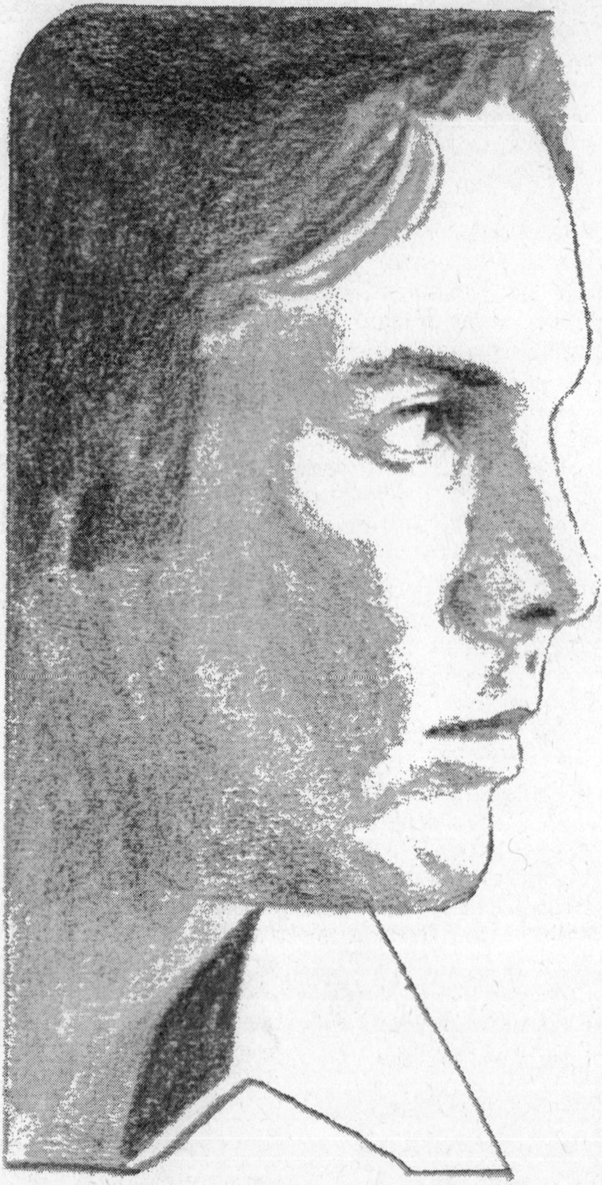

meeting and shared their faith. They told that they had rejected atheism and had received Jesus. All six ended up in a prison camp.

I returned to Dresden not long ago to see how that group of Christians was doing. There a girl told me her story. She had been valedictorian of her high school class before she received Christ and became part of a local body of believers. She had just been told that she couldn't continue her education. She looked at me in tears. Then a big smile crossed her face. "But you know, Sammy," she said, "it is worth it. It's worth it."

All over the world, people are laying down their lives and giving up their freedom, their jobs, their schooling. One third of the world is under atheistic Communism. Yet in many of these countries God's church is alive and well, though suffering. The people that make up the underground body are counting the cost and losing themselves to God for the sake of the faith. In many Islam-dominated countries, Christians suffer persecution. More and more around the world, terrorism, politics, and corruption have become obstacles to Christianity.

In most of the free world, the price of serving God is so little. The cost is cheap, compared with that in other places. No one loses his education for his faith. No one loses his freedom or his life. All that is required of an American, Canadian, or western European Christian is a little time and extra effort. Being a Christian in a free land is nothing compared with the cost to those under strongly non-Christian rule.

When you decide to follow Jesus, you'll see that it'll be worth it. A tremendous blessing is in store for you. Why do you suppose the valedictorian of her class would tell me that losing her education for the sake of Jesus was worth it? Because the joy of serving Jesus outweighs all earthly pleasure and accomplishment.

The greatest joy in my life is found in reproducing and multiplying and seeing my spiritual children—many of them behind the Iron Curtain—beginning to walk with God and disciple others. This is what you have to look forward to when the true discipleship plan of the Scripture runs its full course.

You will go from being a baby to a child and then a young man and then a father. Don't miss the greatest thrill in life, as so many Christians do. Look to the day when you will see your own spiritual babes walk with God, go through rough times, yet remain faithful. Your blessing will be unspeakable (2 Corinthians 9:15). You will experience a deep joy as you see yourself and those you disciple growing in the grace and knowledge of Jesus Christ.

This is my prayer for you: "I have no greater joy than this, to hear of my children walking in the truth" (3 John 4).

SCIPIO UNITED METHODIST